THE JOl CONTINUES

Enchancing Relationships: Your Anchor In Life

VISION
MEDIA COMMUNICATIONS

Unless otherwise stated, all Scripture quotations are from the New King James Version of the Bible. Scripture quotations marked (AMP) are taken from the Amplified Bible. Scripture quotations marked KJV are from the King James Version of the Bible. New International Version, Copyright © 1973, 1978, 1984 by International Bible Society.

Used By Permission

The Journey Continues
Copyright © 2007 by Ade Lawrence-Ojomo
ISBN 978-0-9543745-2-5

Published by
Vision Media Communications Ltd.
Suite 212, 176 Finchley Road
Hampstead, London. NW3 6BT
Mobile: 07903822987
Email: info@developingleaders.net

www.developingleaders.net

Printed in the United Kingdom
Cover design by Ayo Ojomo

ACKNOWLEDGEMENT

The task of writing a book is really a joint effort. As the saying goes, "no one is an island". I would like to thank all those who have always been with me on the journey of life.

The most important crew member on this journey of life – Lola you are a true inspiration.

Gifts acquired along the way from the Almighty God – Afope Rachelle, Ife Danielle and Iyanu Daniel, I could not have asked for anyone else.

Worthy and Blessed vessels that facilitated my entrance into Life – Mum and Dad, loving you always.

Pastor Agu and Sister Ify – I am proud to be your son in the Lord.

Pastor Sola and Sister Funke – thanks for all those crucial nuggets at the right time.

Thanks also to the "spellcheck" trio - Adanna, Morenike and Valerie for your qualitative assessment. Vision Media - for bringing this book to market and Ayo for your graphical interpretation of the title.

To the rest of you, thanks, thanks and an even greater thank you for being along the way.

CONTENTS

PART 1 - RELATIONSHIP WITH GOD

CONTENTS

PART 2 - RELATIONSHIP WITH SELF

CONTENTS

PART 3 - RELATIONSHIP WITH PEOPLE

FOREWORD

This is a clever, thought provoking and topical book – covering issues varying from relating rightly, wisdom and angelic assistance to current affairs, use of time and parenting through to white lies and mission statements – there really is something for everyone.

It approaches the diverse issues innovately and provokes the reader to reflection (and sometimes self-examination). It is a book that will inspire, challenge and encourage you onto growth in every area of your life. I especially liked this part from a section titled 'Baby Talk'.

A disgraced father who had been a public figure asked his son if he felt his (i.e. the son's) life and future career might have better prospects if he was not encumbered with the burden of a disgraced father hovering in the background. His son said "Don't be a chump, Daddy. Even the Guardian can't keep you in the doghouse for ever. You'll find plenty to do. Besides, I need you'. This statement from his son contributed to him not committing suicide and pressing forward to find out God's will for his life. To that I add – Selah!

This book is also easy to read. We live in an age where there are so many demands on our time; and if you are like me you are reading several books at any one time that you don't finish! Ade has written this book in such a way that it's easy to dip in and out of. Instead of chapters, you have just one or two pages to each theme or idea. This makes it easy to readand digest; and great to use as a start to devotions or times of meditation.

I encourage you to buy several copies – keep one in your car (for when you are stuck in traffic), one for the office (to read in your tea break) and one by your bedside (for reflective times). I know your life will be impacted and transformed for good by it. It comes highly recommended.

Enjoy!
Bimbo Fola - Alade

DEDICATION

In memory of

Ify Irukwu and Kehinde (Kenny) Ojeh,

This book is dedicated to you both – the perfect examples of how
to run the race of life which is a gift given to us by the
Almighty God.

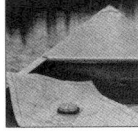

PART I

RELATIONSHIP WITH GOD

ANGELIC ASSISTANCE

For those who are movie buffs, are you not amazed when the main character is trapped in a complex situation and has to fight his way out?

In most cases, that means he has to fight against an army of bad guys, and you are left wondering whether he will survive.

Where were the reinforcements before and during the fight though? The reinforcements always seem to come after the fight has been won by the main character who, by this time, is battered and needs medical attention.

In our fight against the enemy, we sometimes wonder where God is – especially during intense warfare. The good news is that angels are on standby waiting for that command from the Mighty Warrior, as we see in Matthew 4 v10 - 11:

Jesus said to him, "Away from me Satan! For it is written: Worship the Lord your God, and serve him only."
Then the devil left him, and angels came and attended him.

God has guaranteed to give His angels charge over us, lest we dash our feet against a stone. His assurance of protection through angelic assistance is the 'reinforcement' that is always in the wings, waiting for orders from the Lion of the Tribe of Judah.

Praise be to God, that He will never forsake nor leave us!

ANOTHER ONE BITES THE DUST

Dr A.R Bernard spoke about our value system in what I can classify as an insightful message last Sunday.

It got me thinking about the meaning of life in terms of working to make ends meet and be financially comfortable and secure. Also, the lengths to which we go to ensure that we are remunerated to the so called "level of comfort and security".

Question – Is God playing a major role in our pursuit?

Being much wiser after the conference, it is conclusive that our total comfort and security can only be in God – who provides it with a lifetime guarantee.

Revelation 18 v 11 – 14 provides quite a scary insight into the future of the values of a commercial system without God and hence no lifetime guarantee.

The merchants of the earth will weep and mourn over her because no one buys their cargoes any more— cargoes of gold, silver, precious stones and pearls; fine linen, purple, silk and scarlet cloth; every sort of citron wood, and articles of every kind made of ivory, costly wood, bronze, iron and marble; cargoes of cinnamon and spice, of incense, myrrh and frankincense, of wine and olive oil, of fine flour and wheat; cattle and sheep; horses and carriages; and bodies and souls of men. They will say, 'The fruit you longed for is gone from you. All your riches and splendor have vanished, never to be recovered.'

BACK TO THE FUTURE

The constant and endless desire by society to see into the future is evident in the vast amount of money spent on different tools and methods of prediction.

Financial institutions spend millions of dollars designing forecasting models, as they try to predict the direction of that important parameter called interest rates.

The horoscope industry generates millions of interested readers across the globe, as people seek to know the 'good' and 'bad' that lies ahead.

The amounts spent in the gambling industry are enough to wipe out poverty in the world, as people seek to become fortune tellers, investing in attempts to predict the outcome of numerous sporting events.

The lottery has become the latest craze as we are subjected week after week to those famous machines which even have names, as they release the numbered balls that could hold the key to making that 'lucky' person a potential millionaire overnight.

THE CONSTANT AND ENDLESS
DESIRE BY SOCIETY TO SEE INTO THE
FUTURE IS EVIDENT IN THE VAST
AMOUNT OF MONEY SPENT
ON DIFFERENT TOOLS AND
METHODS OF PREDICTION.

Knowing the future is beneficial when the source of information is coming from someone reliable, who has our best interests at heart. The Bible tells us that God is the Alpha and Omega – the beginning and the end. It is therefore wise to seek His counsel for the future and His plan for our lives, since our future lies in Him. We are given an indication of 'future management' in Romans 8 v 26 – 30:

In the same way, the Spirit helps us in our weakness. We do not know what we ought to pray for, but the Spirit himself intercedes for us with groans that words cannot express.

And He who searches our hearts knows the mind of the Spirit, because the Spirit intercedes for the saints in accordance with God's will.

And we know that in all things God works for the good of those who love Him, who have been called according to His purpose.

For those God foreknew He also predestined to be conformed to the likeness of His Son, that He might be the firstborn among many brothers.

And those He predestined, He also called; those He called, He also justified; those He justified, He also glorified.

Orange, the telecoms provider, says 'the future is Orange'; I say 'the future is God'.

COMPLAINTS DEPARTMENT

A popular TV program that encourages customers to report any situation that involves "dodgy" services or products is called "Watch dog". Complaints upon complaints are sent to the TV channel to bring individuals or companies to justice because this has proven to be more effective than launching an attack either orally or written to the complaints departments of these organisations.

As Christians, we have a heavenly "complaints monitoring unit" that listens to our complaints when we pray. We are encouraged to pray about situations rather than complain and backbite to others about the situation. Below are two verses of a hymn by Graham Kendricks and Chris Rolinson which highlight the importance of praying and not complaining:

All Heaven waits with bated breath,
For saints on earth to pray.
Majestic angels ready stand
With swords of fiery blade.
Astounding power awaits a word
From God's resplendent throne.
But God awaits our prayer of faith
That cries "Your will be done"

Awake, O church, arise and pray;
Complaining words discard.
The Spirit comes to fill your mouth

With truth, His mighty sword.
Go place your feet on Satan's ground
And there proclaim Christ's name,
In step with heaven's armies march
To conquer and to reign!

DEFENCE POLICY

"The amount of money spent by nations in shoring up their defence is enough to wipe out global poverty."

My understanding is that this statement was made by a former British Prime Minister.

Even in our personal lives we sometimes erect costly barriers to protect ourselves from people, organisations and even ourselves. There was a time when neighbours were like members of the same family. Nowadays, we cannot send our children to the corner shop to buy a newspaper without fretting!

The government does not help, as all sorts of defensive measures have been drafted in. Some are positive, but quite a number are detrimental to the core values of family life, which is the bedrock of character development.

On the other side of the coin in terms of defence, people will do anything to accept approval and not rejection. This is based on the notion that if you are liked by someone, there is less possibility of being hurt - WRONG!

THERE WAS A TIME WHEN NEIGHBOURS WERE LIKE MEMBERS OF THE SAME FAMILY.

God in his infinite wisdom has advocated the best strategy to apply for defence in Proverbs 16 v 7:

"When a man's ways are pleasing to the LORD He makes even his enemies live at peace with him"

The good thing about this strategic advice is that it does not cost any money – it is free!

DID GOD REALLY SAY?

In my opinion, it is not the amount of the Word you know that makes you effective.

It is the amount of the living Word, revelation and insight that makes a greater impact in our lives. Interpreting the Bible is a very delicate matter because as we know, "the letter killeth".

This means that the literal interpretation of the Bible alone can be misleading, hence the reason we need the guidance of the Holy Spirit to read and apply the Word.

It was revelatory knowledge which stopped David killing Saul in 1 Samuel 24 v 4 - 7:

The men said, "This is the day the LORD spoke of when He said to you, 'I will give your enemy into your hands for you to deal with as you wish.' "Then David crept up unnoticed and cut off a corner of Saul's robe.

Afterward, David was conscience-stricken for having cut off a corner of his robe.

He said to his men, "The LORD forbid that I should do such a thing to my master, the Lord's anointed, or lift my hand against him; for he is the anointed of the LORD ."

With these words David rebuked his men and did not allow them to attack Saul. And Saul left the cave and went his way.

It is so easy to quote Scriptures as a means of justifying our actions, just as David's mighty men did. However, we need to go a step further to confirm what God really did say.

This can be achieved by a deeper walk with God, so He can provide greater insight and revelation of His Word through the guidance of the Holy Spirit.

That was how David knew the correct way to treat the Lord's anointed.

DISARMAMENT TREATY

"We the people who have been elected and chosen to govern the nations on the Earth, in order to eliminate and reduce the possibility and severity of wars, do agree to this Global Disarmament Treaty so that nations and human beings may settle their conflicts in peace and with justice according to universal laws that are fair for all without the intervention of armed force"

This treaty was signed by global leaders in their efforts to promote world peace.

Recently the UK adopted a similar approach in their efforts to reduce rampant gun and knife crimes amongst the youth. People were encouraged to drop their weapons at the nearest police station without being charged.

In my opinion – these attempts are good but they do not address the root cause of the problem at hand. A greater force is needed to attack the root and eliminate its cause and effect forever.

This force is seen in Colossians 2 v 13 – 15:

When you were dead in your sins and in the uncircumcision of your sinful nature, God made you alive with Christ. He forgave us all our sins, having cancelled the written code, with its regulations, that was against us and that stood opposed to us; He took it away, nailing it to the cross. And having disarmed the powers and authorities,

He made a public spectacle of them, triumphing over them by the cross.

If the people humble themselves and begin to pray then the world will be disarmed of global terror and carnage.

DISASTER RECOVERY PLAN

As a result of the potential attacks by terrorists on their key strategic location, organisations have drafted and implemented plans to facilitate "going concern". In other words - contingency plans are written and communicated to the key decision makers of these locations to ensure that once an attack occurs - operations are transferred with minimal interruption to the disaster recovery centres.

We see an example in 1 Samuel 30 v 7 - 8, as David implements his own disaster recovery procedure after a devastating attack on Ziklag:

Then David said to Abiathar the priest, the son of Ahimelech, "Bring me the ephod." Abiathar brought it to him, and David inquired of the LORD, "Shall I pursue this raiding party? Will I overtake them?" "Pursue them," He answered. "You will certainly overtake them and succeed in the rescue."

We see the effectiveness of the plans highlighted in 1 Samuel 30 v 18 - 19:

David recovered everything the Amalekites had taken, including his two wives. Nothing was missing: young or old, boy or girl, plunder or anything else they had taken. David brought everything back.

DO THE RIGHT THING!

It would be terrible to get to heaven to find out that all we thought was right was actually wrong and not in line with God's overall plan!

How do you know you are doing the right thing?

It is so easy to assume that we are righteous because we go to church, and that every decision we make is correct because it makes sense. Are we still confident when God's answers and ways do not seem to make sense?

In Matthew 1 v 19 – 21, we see an example where God uses a virgin to bring His Son into the world. In my opinion, Joseph's reaction was mild compared to what most of us would have done. Thank God for the intervention of the Holy Spirit:

"Because Joseph her husband was a righteous man and did not want to expose her to public disgrace, he had in mind to divorce her quietly.

But after he had considered this, an angel of the Lord appeared to him in a dream and said, "Joseph son of

David, do not be afraid to take Mary home as your wife, because what is conceived in her is from the Holy Spirit".

IT WOULD BE TERRIBLE TO GET TO HEAVEN TO FIND OUT THAT ALL WE THOUGHT WAS RIGHT WAS ACTUALLY WRONG AND NOT IN LINE WITH GOD'S OVERALL PLAN!

She will give birth to a son, and you are to give him the name Jesus, because he will save his people from their sins."

When the Bible points out that His ways are not our ways, it reinforces the fact that God is sovereign and He decides what is right and wrong.

David was a murderer – yet God declared that he was a man after His heart. Tamar was a prostitute – yet she was part of the Jesus' genealogy. Job was presumably righteous but lost all his wealth and children, only to be restored later as a result of God's mercy.

We need to ask ourselves how we would have reacted in the scenarios above, and we can safely conclude that God's ultimate wisdom is required to do the right thing!

EVERYBODY MAKE SOME NOISE

The scene was set; the two convicted men were paraded in front of the mob that consisted of two groups of people.

Some were rooting for the first victim, while 'the others' were rooting for the second in a rather timid way. The general in charge of declaring judgment knew he had a hard task and was confused, particularly as his wife had warned him not to get involved because of a dream she had the previous night.

In my opinion, because of his status as a general, he had to save face and succumb to the wishes of the people by allowing them to choose who would be set free.

'Who do you want to be set free?' echoed the general and to his amazement the loudest cries were for victim one, the Al Capone of this era. The cries for victim two were not even heard, even though he was so innocent that the general could not find any reason to execute him. Hence he washed his hands off the matter after giving his judgment.

The Bible highlights the consequences of being ashamed of Jesus in Mark 8 v 38:

If anyone is ashamed of me and my words in this adulterous and sinful generation, the Son of Man will be ashamed of him when he comes in his Father's glory with the holy angels."

How many times are we told to stand up for Jesus and proclaim the gospel with boldness? If we remain silent like 'the others' people will not be set free, and will be condemned to a life of misery.

Like those who shouted with such boldness that the general had no choice but to free 'Al Capone', let us raise our voices and proclaim the name of Jesus to set the captives free.

EXCHANGE AND MART

Trading by barter primarily involves the exchange of products and/or services.

It is normally based on people's different preferences, as they exchange one item for another that appears to be of more benefit. The success of an effective barter trade can be measured by the degree of satisfaction of both parties.

The Bible gives an example of a barter trade that is not beneficial to the body of Christ in Romans 1 v 25:

They exchanged the truth of God for a lie, and worshiped and served created things rather than the Creator – who is forever praised. Amen.

What do we do with the product called the "truth of God" in our daily lives? Do we exchange it for selfish personal beliefs, negative attitudes, pride, unwholesome values and sinful lifestyles, or do we exchange it for righteousness, peace and joy in the Holy Ghost?

The exchanges we make in life have to be made in the light of the best standards found in the Word of God. This is what provides satisfaction and contentment.

FEAR FACTOR

At a discussion forum on the topic of Change Management, a participant pointed out that people resist change because of the 'fear of the unknown'

This phrase is a very interesting one, and you may ask yourself what they are scared of, seeing as it is unknown?

This raises the issue of how to get from the unknown to the known, so we are not fearful.

Successful companies constantly plan and implement diverse scenario analysis to make provision for possible changes that may occur in the future, to reduce the 'fear factor'. As a result of this exercise, the companies are equipped with information to reduce the risk of the unknown.

God has also assured us that fear does not come from Him in 2 Timothy 1 v 7:

He has not given us a spirit of fear but of power, love and a sound mind.

God is not caught unawares. If we are confused or unsure of any situation, let us seek the required information from the Word of God. As that famous Scripture says in John 8 v 32:

"Then you will know the truth, and the truth will set you free."

FEARLESS

Reading Psalm 5 this morning kept me pondering over the subject of reverential fear of God. How do we truly have godly respect and fear for the Almighty God?

When we look at the way we respect and fear people from the Pastors in our church to world dignitaries like the Presidents, Kings and Queens – why do we sometimes struggle to fear God in an unlimited measure?

Could it be that we truly lack the understanding of godly fear or do we fear people because we are forced to or is it driven by motive?

I truly do not know the full answers to these questions but I feel it is a subject that as Christians we need to get to grips with because to fear God is much more than saying with our mouths – "I truly fear God". Also when we consider some of our actions when dealing with God comparable to people we often wonder – who is truly God in our lives?

In my search for true knowledge, understanding and wisdom on this subject, I took my initial lecture from Proverbs 2 v 1 – 5:

TO FEAR GOD
IS MUCH MORE THAN
SAYING WITH OUR MOUTHS –
'I TRULY FEAR GOD'.

My son, if you receive my words, And treasure my commands within you, So that you incline your ear to wisdom, And apply your heart to understanding; Yes, if you cry out for discernment, And lift up your voice for understanding, If you seek her as silver, And search for her as for hidden treasures; Then you will understand the fear of the LORD, And find the knowledge of God.

FORTUNE 100 RICH LIST

To be honest, I have been amongst those who have queued up to read the "much awaited" names of the 100 richest people in the world. A secret thought passes through your mind that you will be content with even being number one hundred when you consider the amount of wealth on display.

You think that if you could just have 0.1 % of the wealth of Rich List number one hundred – then you are sorted. Mortgage paid off, kids to the best private schools, ten percent to the church (and even more!), donation to charities "etcetera, etcetera, etcetera" – if I may borrow the phrase of the King of Saigon in the film "The King and I!"

Michael Douglas in the film "Wall Street" advised the business school students that "greed is good" but he should have read what the Bible says about riches in Proverbs 11 v 4:

IN GOD WE MUST TRUST AND NOT RICHES!

"Riches do not profit in the day of wrath, but righteousness delivers from death"

FREAKY FRIDAY

Those of you with children (particularly girls) may have been subjected to watching a film called Freaky Friday.

That would have been the case if you have Sky TV and one digibox. It does not matter the number of televisions you own - you can only watch one channel at a time!

The film is about a mother and daughter who exchange identities through an out-of-body experience. As a result, each begins to learn and experience what the other goes through on a daily basis. By the end of the film, the respect they had for each other had grown.

On the way to church yesterday, a man got on the train looking drunk and badly battered. He was in such a state, with bloodshot eyes and rough attire. As I began to think about the film 'Freaky Friday' a scary thought emerged, about me and this guy going through the same process! It was at Camden Station that the scary thought was broken, when the man got off the train.

Paul reminds us that if not for the grace of God, we could all easily be that man on the train. This reminder is in 1 Timothy 1 v 12 – 14:

I thank Christ Jesus our Lord, who has given me strength, that he considered me faithful, appointing me to his service.

Even though I was once a blasphemer and a persecutor and a violent man, I was shown mercy because I acted in ignorance and unbelief.

The grace of our Lord was poured out on me abundantly, along with the faith and love that are in Christ Jesus.

This grace is what enables us to love everyone, regardless of their situation.

HANDOVER PROCEDURES

On my way to church last Sunday, I began to ponder as I saw the masses of people veering in different directions to accomplish their tasks for the day.

The thought that some of these people will not go to heaven because they have not accepted Jesus as their personal

Saviour became alarmingly worrying. I began to question why our main focus as Christians tends to be our own personal issues, which clutter our minds and act as a major detriment to our witnessing capabilities.

The Holy Spirit interrupted my session of 'deep thought' by reminding me of a process at work called 'The Handover Process'.

For example, this could involve transferring the responsibility for an IT computer system to the client on completion, thereby allowing you to focus your resources on other projects. In other words, we should release all our personal issues onto our major client - God - and focus on witnessing and sharing the Gospel.

It was amazing how the sermon for that day later confirmed the importance of witnessing.

God's 'handover procedure' is highlighted in 1 Peter 5 v 7:

Cast all your anxiety on Him because He cares for you.

Hand over all your concerns to God to release the capacity to witness the Gospel, and to reduce the tendency to focus on self.

THE THOUGHT THAT SOME OF THESE PEOPLE WILL NOT GO TO HEAVEN BECAUSE THEY HAVE NOT ACCEPTED JESUS AS THEIR PERSONAL SAVIOUR BECAME ALARMINGLY WORRYING

HIDE AND SEEK

In the film Enemy of the State, Will Smith's character tried to outrun the CIA, but to no avail.

Technology provided the means to capture every word, thought and deed implemented by Mr. Smith. I have been told that providing information on the internet is an open license to others to tour our private lives.

Why are we bothered if we are doing the right thing and have nothing to hide?

What we should be bothered about is not being monitored by man, but by God. His technology far outweighs any gadgets employed by the CIA, FBI or any other secret service organization. In Psalm 139 v 8 – 12, the Bible makes clear the omnipresent capabilities of our Mighty God;

If I ascend up into heaven, You are there; if I make my bed in Sheol (the place of the dead), behold, You are there.

If I take the wings of the morning or dwell in the uttermost parts of the sea,

Even there shall Your hand lead me, and Your right hand shall hold me.

Even the darkness hides nothing from You, but the night shines as the day; the darkness and the light are both alike to You.

The scope of God's surveillance is wide and penetrates any physical barrier. In conclusion, we ought to remember that famous phrase, 'You can run, but you can't hide!'

ICBM

In this case I am not referring to the name of a company, but to the phrase 'Intercontinental Ballistic Missile'.

ICBMs are arsenals of powerful nuclear weapons that can cause so much damage, that during the Cold War every country desired to hold them to deter potential attacks from enemy nations. One cannot underestimate the awesome power contained within one nuclear head and the havoc it could wreak.

Imagine all that power within one entity. The Bible tells us that we also have so much power within us. In fact, it says greater is the power within us than that in the world. This means that sin - which is our enemy - should be afraid of the potential damage this power can do when demonstrated. Hebrews 4 v 12 gives us a further description of its havoc on sin:

For the word of God is quick, and powerful, and sharper than any two edged sword, piercing even to the dividing asunder of soul and spirit, and of the joints and marrow, and is a discerner of the thoughts and intents of the heart.

Let us use the power of the Word within us to counter any attack from the enemy of sin in our lives.

IDENTITY CRISIS

Two important questions we need to ask ourselves on a regular basis are:

1. *Who am I?*
2. *Where am I from?*

Having the right answers to these questions helps make us secure, as long as those answers are based on the truth. So much confusion about the origin of man has led to theories such as Darwin's and the Big Bang.

Fraudsters who steal other people's identities really do not understand the implications behind their actions. They have no idea and do not care about the history of the person, but one day they will steal the identity of someone who has a very negative credit history and by so doing, find themselves in troubled waters.

Seeking the answers to these two questions has also led people to spend loads of money researching their family trees to trace their roots. Romans 1 v 2 - 4 gives us an insight into our origins and who we are in Christ, as it tells us the origin of Christ in terms of His human and spiritual nature:

The gospel He promised beforehand through His prophets in the Holy Scriptures.

Regarding His Son, who as to His human nature was a descendant of David,

And who through the Spirit of holiness was declared with power to be the Son of God by His resurrection from the dead: Jesus Christ our Lord.

We all have human ancestors, but we should remember that our spiritual ancestry is in God through His Son Jesus.

INHERITANCE TAX

There was a time in this country when I could not even open a bank account without going through the equivalent of a "FBI or CIA" security check. Once I bought a house, the offers came flooding through the post at such an alarming rate that you would think that the bank manager and myself were on first name basis and we shared golfing tips at the local fairway

With the approval of the mortgage came the invasion of the banks' "marketing crew" as they guaranteed me all the promises in the world just to sign the dotted line giving them the "right" and the "access" to use my deposited funds in return for an attractive interest.

I wonder how the customers of Lloyds, Enron, Barings and many other financial institutions felt when life threw them the dreaded "curve ball" to enhance the fact that nothing is effectively guaranteed except the inheritance given by Jesus Christ. This is eloquently pointed out by Paul in Ephesians 1 v 13 -14:

And you also were included in Christ when you heard the word of truth, the gospel of your salvation. Having believed, you were marked in Him with a seal, the promised Holy Spirit, who is a deposit guaranteeing our inheritance until the redemption of those who are God's possession—to the praise of His glory.

Investing in a relationship with Jesus Christ will give you a guaranteed return which even the moths can't invade!

INVISIBLE MAN

Car lovers are ecstatic when they see a well built vehicle cruising down the autobahn at speeds which sometimes defies the "laws of road gravity". Formula 1 enthusiasts will even take you up the "knowledge curve" of the "ins" and "outs" of the drivers and team championship set up. By the time they finish describing the sleekness of the cars, you will think that there is a love relationship between them.

In both cases, the excitement is based on what you see but what really determines the uniqueness of the cars cannot really be seen. The uniqueness is based on the engine which is sealed up in a compartment, hidden from the view of the admirers. Hence the reason why to truly assess a car, you should look at the engine because a car may have the sleekest body but underneath it has a substandard engine.

The importance of assessment based on internals is also highlighted in 2 Corinthians 4 v 17 - 18:

For our light and momentary troubles are achieving for us an eternal glory that far outweighs them all. So we fix our eyes not on what is seen, but on what is unseen. For what is seen is temporary, but what is unseen is eternal.

Remember the saying "All that glitters is not gold".

IT'S BONUS TIME

When I worked on the trading floor of an Investment Bank, December was a wonderful time for the traders depending on your perceived level of contribution and commitment to the organisation. You always knew the period in December when it came to pass based on the smiles or frowns that you received when you went to the traders to source trading information

This was a period when a lot of politics was played on the trading floor to be in the "good books" of the "distributor" who was normally the Head Trader. The distributor as the name implies has the freedom to rationalise the allocation as he saw fit hence the hustling, jostling and strategic manoeuvres as one would perform during a chess game.

Romans 2 v 7 -11, highlights a more influential "distributor" who also awards an everlasting type of "bonus" which does not depend on hustling, jostling or political wrangling – but on you, by his grace remaining in his "good books":

God will give to each person according to what he has done. To those who by persistence in doing good seek glory, honor and immortality, He will give eternal life. But for those who are self-seeking and who reject the truth and follow evil, there will be wrath and anger. There will be trouble and distress for every human being who does evil: first for the Jew, then for the Gentile; but glory, honor and peace for everyone who does good: first for the Jew, then for the Gentile. For God does not show favouritism.

Let us seek to be good at all times without getting weary for in His time, He will reward us.

JACK OF ALL TRADES – MASTER OF NONE

The world has become so complex and busy, and the enemy has used this to distract us and stop us concentrating on 'that one thing' *which is important.*

In the film *City Slickers,* the cowboy assigned to train the three yuppies pointed out that "you city slickers focus on too many things; I advise you to find that one thing that means something."

In the bestselling book *Good to Great,* the author Jim Collins describes an ancient Greek parable about a hedgehog and a fox. The fox uses different strategies in an attempt to destroy the hedgehog, but on each occasion the hedgehog wonders if the fox will ever learn, as he becomes a sphere of sharp spikes pointing outwards in all directions.

The author draws from this parable the analogy that people are divided into two basic groups. Foxes pursue many ends at the same time and see the world in all its complexity – never integrating their thinking into one overall concept or unifying vision. Hedgehogs, on the other hand, simplify a complex world into a single organised idea, a basic principle or concept that unifies and guides everything.

Jesus was an expert in simplifying issues, as we see in how He handled the question posed by the Pharisees regarding the commandments in Mark 12 v 28 – 30:

One of the teachers of the law came and heard them debating. Noticing that Jesus had given them a good answer, he asked him, "Of all the commandments, which is the most important?"

"The most important one" answered Jesus, "is this: 'Hear, O Israel, the Lord our God, the Lord is one.

Love the Lord your God with all your heart and with all your soul and with all your mind and with all your strength.'

As pointed out in numerous examples in the book *Good to Great* – it is refreshing to see a company succeed so brilliantly by taking one simple concept and just doing it with excellence and imagination.

Love is 'that one thing' which we need to carry out with excellence and imagination.

JUDGMENT DAY

I am not talking about the film Terminator 2: Judgment Day, but about that day when we will face our Maker, God Almighty.

The finality of death was illustrated in a recent message by a pastor who had a near-death experience, and was told by an angel that it was time to go home. He began to think about his family and ministry, and pointed out to the angel that he had not yet finished his assignment on earth. God's mercy and grace took over, as he was given a second chance to go and fulfill his assignment.

On this occasion grace and mercy took over, but sometimes it does not, and we will all have to make that final journey eventually. The importance of taking our assignments from God seriously and living a life free of sin is brought home in Hebrews 9 v 27:

Just as man is destined to die once, and after that to face judgment

In the film, Arnold Schwarzenegger had the luxury of saying, "I'll be back!" In reality, this luxury does not exist since once we die; the next major milestone is the judgment when we face the Almighty Judge of Heaven and Earth.

In Jesus' name, when we say "I'll be back", let it be when our bodies are transformed and our spirits renewed in His glory, because we have fulfilled our assignments and been approved by the Lamb of God.

KNOWING YOU JESUS

Did you know that it is possible to live with someone and yet not truly know the person? Couples go through years and years of marriage; people work side by side with their colleagues in the same organization for years; Pastors minister to the same congregation for years – not knowing the congregation and the congregation not knowing the Pastor.

There is a potential danger in not taking the time to know those you associate with. This arises from the fact that when they do something out of the ordinary whether good or bad you won't be able to vouch for the individual's character or confirm the feasibility of the individual being able to perform certain activities.

When I released my first book called "On the Move", even some of my close friends did not believe that I wrote it as the phrase "which O.J?" rang through the grapevine. Those that actually gave me positive feedback in terms of my potential to write a book were those that I only communicated with via "Tips for the Day".

The good news is that we are not alone as we see that the disciples of Jesus fell into the same boat as confirmed in Luke 8 verse 24 – 25 despite their association with Jesus:

The disciples went and woke him, saying, "Master, Master, we're going to drown!" He got up and rebuked the wind and the raging waters; the storm subsided, and all was calm. "Where is your faith?" He asked His disciples. In fear and amazement they asked one another, "Who is this? He commands even the winds and the water, and they obey him."

BUT WHAT ABOUT YOU? HE ASKED. WHO DO YOU SAY I AM? PETER ANSWERED, THE CHRIST OF GOD.

They called him Master but they did not truly know Him as one who had total control over the Universe. Later in Luke 9 v 18 – 20, we see Peter finally getting a true knowledge of Christ:

Once when Jesus was praying in private and His disciples were with Him, He asked them, "Who do the crowds say I am?" They replied, "Some say John the Baptist; others say Elijah; and still others, that one of the prophets of long ago has come back to life." "But what about you?"

He asked. "Who do you say I am?" Peter answered, "The Christ of God."

To really know someone we need to take the time with God's assistance to study and observe so we make the right assessment.

KNOWLEDGE CURVE

I am currently working on a project where I replaced an independent contractor who had limited knowledge on implementing the proposed system. As a result of this, the analysis and design was based on inaccurate information.

My first task involved doing due diligence prior to commencing the build phase and I found out that some of the major recommendations were wrong. The client was not impressed and since the "former expert" had left - who bears the brunt of the handiwork? - "yours truly". This resulted in the phrase that most children are acquainted with being levied at the project team on a regular basis - "Why"?

I felt rather uncomfortable at the questions to the stage that I even found it uncomfortable to answer and it began to occupy my mind - even during my prayer time. There was a reason for this as the Lord queried me as to why I was uncomfortable if I knew the answers and if not, I should go to His database - a.k.a "The Word" for the right answer.

I took the instruction to heart and found my answer in James 1 v 5 - 8:

If any of you lacks wisdom, he should ask God, who gives generously to all without finding fault, and it will be given to him. But when he asks, he must believe and not doubt, because he who doubts is like a wave of the sea, blown and tossed by the wind. That man should not think he will receive anything from the Lord; he is a double-minded man, unstable in all he does.

Thank God for the stability that comes from His "Database".

LET US PRAY

The meeting is well under way, we have worshiped, praised, danced and laughed, and the time comes when the pastor says, 'Let us pray!'

This is when we hope that all our prayer points are addressed in one form or the other.

Have any of you felt that the phrases 'Let us pray' and 'What are the prayer points?' sometimes sound like clichés? How may times have you found yourself telling someone that you will be praying for them, only to promptly forget?

The entire concept of prayer should be taken more seriously, because it is every Christian's lifeline. It is the fuel that facilitates the accomplishment of God's will for our lives. This concept is reinforced in Colossians 1 v 9 – 12:

For this reason, since the day we heard about you, we have not stopped praying for you and asking God to fill you with the knowledge of His will through all spiritual wisdom and understanding.

And we pray this in order that you may live a life worthy of the Lord and may please Him in every way: bearing fruit in every good work, growing in the knowledge of God, being strengthened with all power according to his glorious might so that you may have great endurance and patience, and joyfully giving thanks to the Father, who has qualified you to share in the inheritance of the saints in the kingdom of light.

As you can see from the Scriptures above, there is a lot to be gained from effective and sincere prayer.

MILITARY INTELLIGENCE

What wins the war for a country is the accuracy of the information that gets to its troops.

The issue is certainly not with the amount of information, as modern technology has ensured that there are numerous sources for both true and false information, as seen during the Second World War when false propaganda was spread to demoralise the enemy army and encourage the home troops.

What sets a commanding officer apart is how he analyses and filters all the information through to his troops to guarantee victory. This is so crucial that all United States army personnel at war are equipped with communications gear in their helmets, so they can be kept abreast of developments.

This same principle needs to be applied during spiritual warfare. In engaging with the enemy, we need to know the right words to say and apply. Binding, Loosing, Fasting, and Deliverance are sometimes applied in situations where different solutions are required. This is where our Helper plays an important role, as pointed out in John 14 v 25 - 26:

All this I have spoken while still with you. But the Counselor, the Holy Spirit, whom the Father will send in my name, will teach you all things and will remind you of everything I have said to you.

Every word Jesus spoke came from God. He pointed out in verse 24 of the same chapter that the words He spoke belonged to the Father who had sent Him.

The intelligence we need in 'our helmets' to engage in effective warfare comes from the Helper. The Holy Spirit will ensure that the right word of Scripture is applied in the right situation. We need to refrain from 'machine gun' type warfare and engage in effective and direct warfare. This is what guarantees results.

MIND THE GAP

The dictionary defines a gap as "An opening in a structure or surface; a cleft or breach".

In most cases, gaps represent any exposure that makes us vulnerable to impending attack from the enemy. Hence the reason we are advised not to create any 'gaps' or 'openings' in the armour of God.

Managers of football teams and military commanders understand the need to eliminate gaps in their strategies, hence the constant change of team formations in terms of attack and defence. The impact of presenting such an exposure can be seen in Joshua 8 v 16 -19:

All the men of Ai were called to pursue them, and they pursued Joshua and were lured away from the city. Not a man remained in Ai or Bethel who did not go after Israel. They left the city open and went in pursuit of Israel.

Then the LORD said to Joshua, "Hold out toward Ai the javelin that is in your hand, for into your hand I will deliver the city." So Joshua held out his javelin toward Ai.

As soon as he did this, the men in the ambush rose quickly from their position and rushed forward. They entered the city and captured it and quickly set it on fire.

We need to not only 'mind the gap'; we need to eliminate the gaps in our defences to prevent the enemy from getting a stronghold in our lives.

MIND YOUR LANGUAGE

One of the most controversial issues surrounding the church is the speaking of tongues. In my opinion the issue lies around the question:

What you are talking about?

Message upon message highlights the fact that "speaking in tongues" is a heavenly language that is facilitated by the assistance of the Holy Spirit but like all languages – surely interpretation is required?

We are encouraged that speaking in tongue edifies the individual but prophesying or interpretation edifies the church and is greater because there is clarity and understanding of the delivered message.

After reading some scriptures on this topic, I became quite worried about the amount of years I have been speaking in tongue edifying myself and how it would be nice to extend this to the body of Christ. Thank God for His grace and understanding as He steered me to 1 Corinthians 14 v 8 – 13 on how to acquire the gift of interpretation.

Again, if the trumpet does not sound a clear call, who will get ready for battle? So it is with you. Unless you speak intelligible words with your tongue, how will anyone know what you are saying? You will just be speaking into the air. Undoubtedly there are all sorts of

languages in the world, yet none of them is without meaning. If then I do not grasp the meaning of what someone is saying, I am a foreigner to the speaker, and he is a foreigner to me. So it is with you. Since you are eager to have spiritual gifts, try to excel in gifts that build up the church. For this reason anyone who speaks in a tongue should pray that he may interpret what he says.

As the scripture points out – let us pray earnestly for the gift of interpretation which is available for all so that apart from edifying ourselves – we can extend this benefit to the body of Christ.

MISSION IMPOSSIBLE

Breaking News!

1. Sadaam Hussein has declared his ultimate love for Jesus Christ by giving his life in a crusade hosted by Osama Bin Laden;
2. Tears of Joy as thousands of youths hand over their knives and guns after the demonstration of God's power on the Grahame Park Estate in Colindale;
3. Amazing scenes at the Nigeria 2007 elections as the losing parties all lift up hands in unity praying for the new leader;
4. All Jews unite as they all accept that Jesus Christ was truly the Messiah who was sent to facilitate their salvation.

You think that you heard it all until you get home and your bride-to-be pays you a visit and informs you that she is pregnant. As the Senior Pastor of a thriving church this is surely a wind-up considering she still stays with her parents!

Be honest everyone, do you believe that all this can happen? The good news is that this can happen as confirmed by the events described in Luke 1 v 34 – 37:

How will this be," Mary asked the angel, "since I am a virgin?" The angel answered, "The Holy Spirit will come upon you, and the power of the Most High will overshadow you. So the holy one to be born will be called the Son of God. Even Elizabeth your relative is going to have a child in her old age, and she who was said to be barren is in her sixth month. For nothing is impossible with God."

God is the Ultimate – if he says it will come to pass, you can take it to the bank!

MURDER SHE WROTE

The title above is based on a popular television series in which a novelist continuously assumes the role of private investigator.

Books are written to educate and enlighten us on events that go on around us. They can either be based on real-life events, or on fictional occurrences. The Bible, on the other hand, is based on the truth, but there is another dimension to this great book that we need to consider, else we risk classifying it as just a great story book.

Even the Sanhedrin understood the impact of this power, and we see them commanding Peter and John in Acts 4 v18 not to mention the name of Jesus. This is reinforced in 1 Thessalonians 1 v 4 - 5, where Paul explains the origin of the gospel to the people:

For we know, brothers loved by God, that he has chosen you, because our gospel came to you not simply with words, but also with power, with the Holy Spirit and with deep conviction. You know how we lived among you for your sake.

I now understand why Bible knowledge was just a subject in secondary school, and not a sermon! We need the power of the Holy Spirit behind every word that proceeds from this great book.

MYSTIC MEG

My judgmental attitude got hold of me as I watched a chat show on Ben TV yesterday.

The topic was horoscopes, and viewers could send in their opinions. Someone pointed out that the practice was ungodly, and that only God knows our future. In response, one of the panellists who claimed to be a Christian said there was nothing wrong with it, citing the three wise men as examples of people in the Bible who had used astronomy as a tool in their quest to find where the baby Jesus lay.

On my way to drop my children at school my Counsellor, the Holy Spirit pointed out that the panellist had given her views according to her level of knowledge, and she needed to be exposed to the light that comes from the Word of God.

He also reminded me that I would also have been in darkness, but for the grace and light that comes from God. As is His manner, He pointed me to a passage of Scripture in Ephesians 5 v 8 -14:

For you were once darkness, but now you are light in the Lord. Live as children of light (for the fruit of the light consists in all goodness, righteousness and truth) and find out what pleases the Lord.

Have nothing to do with the fruitless deeds of darkness, but rather expose them. For it is shameful even to mention what the disobedient do in secret. But everything exposed by the light becomes visible, for it is light that makes everything visible. This is why it is said: "Wake up, O sleeper, rise from the dead, and Christ will shine on you."

May the Word of God be a lamp unto our feet and a light unto our path.

NOTHING JUST HAPPENS

One of the best pieces of advice I received when I joined a consulting firm was from a senior partner.

He pointed out that one should never assume anything. In other words, make enquiries and try to find the root causes of and solution to a problem, rather than assume you have all the answers. Hence, we see enquiry after enquiry being made after major events to determine the root causes and, in some cases, to satisfy human curiosity.

It is a dangerous concept to assume anything, especially if there is a repeated pattern. If the generations of your family have always been in debt or involved in divorce, for example, there is a reason. You should try to find out the causes and uproot them.

There was a repeated pattern in 2 Samuel 21 v 1; a pattern of repeated famine. In order to find the root cause, David sought the face of the LORD:

During the reign of David, there was a famine for three successive years; so David sought the face of the LORD. The LORD said, "It is on account of Saul and his blood-stained house; it is because he put the Gibeonites to death."

Nothing just happens, so it is dangerous to assume that we know the root cause of an event or situation. Following on from the advice of my senior partner, never assume, but make enquiries by seeking the face of the LORD God Almighty.

PAY DAY

29th, 30th or the 31st are common days associated with the inflow of funds into our bank accounts. We look forward to these days to either increase or decrease our net worth as we seek to replace the money that we have spent ahead of time – in other words "credit".

The inflow of funds is a reward for all the work that we have performed for our employers. Now for employees that have done exceptionally well, a term called "bonus" may be an additional reward for outstanding work depending on the feedback from your boss to the "powers that be".

As mentioned earlier, pay day could be on any of these three days, but in the future – there will be one day "only" that is associated with the pay and bonus of everyone. That day is called "judgment day" as described in Revelation 20 v 11 – 15:

Then I saw a great white throne and Him who was seated on it. Earth and sky fled from His presence, and there was no place for them. And I saw the dead, great and small, standing before the throne, and books were opened. Another book was opened, which is the book of life. The dead were judged according to what they had

done as recorded in the books. The sea gave up the dead that were in it, and death and Hades gave up the dead that were in them, and each person was judged according to what he had done. Then death and Hades were thrown into the lake of fire. The lake of fire is the second death. If anyone's name was not found written in the book of life, he was thrown into the lake of fire.

May the Holy Spirit guide and prepare us for that eventful day.

PRAYER SCHOOL

The *Discipleship Journal* published an article highlighting that our prayers as leaders must be strategic. It pointed out that prayer can be of three kinds:

1. Logistical prayer – We pray logistically when we ask God for the small things: "Lord, help the microphones to work today as I teach."
2. Tactical prayer – We pray tactically when we pray for more meaningful things, but still not for the ultimate: "Lord. Help me to say something meaningful today to my people."
3. Strategic prayer – We pray strategically when we pray or the ultimate purposes of God: "Lord, may You be glorified today and may You raise up disciples from this meeting."

We see an example of God's response to a strategic prayer in 2 Kings 3 v 16 – 18, to the people of Israel, Judah and Edom when they ran out of water.

And he said, this is what the Lord says, make this valley full of ditches. For this is what the LORD says: You will see neither wind nor rain, yet this valley will be filled with water, and you, your cattle and your other animals will drink. This is an easy thing in the eyes of the LORD; he will also hand Moab over to you.

Every thing is easy for God to do; we just need to connect to him with the right prayer requests.

PRESIDENT FOR LIFE

If only the subject of the title could be true. We have seen numerous examples of dictators that assume leadership positions and confer themselves with this title.

No position in life is permanent as the world is not a stagnant environment – people must move on to better things. The mark of a great leader is to hand over a favourable position to his incumbent.

Your leadership tenure should be for an appointed time and period and not for eternity - it is not possible physically anyway!

The only person that is a true "President for Life" is Jesus Christ as highlighted in Ephesians 1 v 20

Now He is far above any ruler or authority or power or leader or anything else—not only in this world but also in the world to come. God has put all things under the authority of Christ and has made Him head over all things for the benefit of the church.

YOUR LEADERSHIP TENURE SHOULD BE FOR AN APPOINTED TIME AND PERIOD AND NOT FOR ETERNITY

PUBLIC OPINION POLL

I am amazed at the amount of opinion polls that are held today to obtain people's view on nearly every issue from "Should Charles marry Camilla" to "Should the FIFA golden ball trophy be taken away from Zidane".

We have all heard the expression "there is always one" – in other words there will always be an awkward, difficult, negative person that you have to work with on a team. I have recently joined a new project and straight away the "public opinion poll" machinery went into action as they began to give me their opinions about a particular member of the team.

Later in the day, I began to ponder on their comments and asked myself why the statement – "there is always one" can't mean someone who is not ready to compromise a "status quo" of holiness, godliness, moral standing and a positive character trait. One thing is certain in life – you can not satisfy all of the people all of the time.

So what do we do? – The answer is simple as highlighted in John 3 v 16 - focus on what God thinks about his children. It is his opinion that counts and not that of "people".

"For God so loved the world that He gave His one and only Son, that whoever believes in Him shall not perish but have eternal life.

People's opinions are like a wave that goes up and down – remember what they said about Jesus! One day they shouted "Son of David!" and the next they shouted "Crucify Him!"

REVELATION T.V.

During the Falklands war, it was suggested that the Americans assisted the British Troops with a lot of intelligence which outlined the strategic positioning of the Argentine fleet. This was achieved through the aid of their Global Positioning Satellites a.k.a. GPS

This technology which was barely available years ago can be downloaded via the click of the button on the internet and the software integrated into a Personal Digital Assistance

(P.D.A). I particularly like the word "Personal' because it can be aligned with the words intimacy, care and friendliness.

This was what the American were to the British as the competitive advantage provided via the GPS ensured that the initial "fighter plan re-fuelling" disadvantages the British troops had because of the long distance from the UK to the island was eliminated. The revelation of enemy location facilitated effective decision making and the effective mobilisation of British troops.

The advantages of "inside knowledge" a.k.a. revelation, is highlighted in Amos 3 v 7:

"Surely the Lord God will do nothing, but He revealeth his secret unto His servants the prophets"

A relationship with God will ensure that the right co-ordinates are keyed into your personal G.P.S for effective decision making and action.

ROUTE PLANNER

You get in the car and punch the co-ordinates of your journey into the GPS navigator.

One of the options on the menu gives you the ability to choose from the fastest or shortest routes, and also warns of impending road blocks, accidents, and road works.

God has His own guiding system in the form of the Holy Spirit and angels, and sometimes, through dreams. Evidence of its use is seen in Matthew 2 v 12 – 15:

And having been warned in a dream not to go back to Herod, they returned to their country by another route. When they had gone, an angel of the Lord appeared to Joseph in a dream. "Get up," he said, "take the child and his mother and escape to Egypt. Stay there until I tell you, for Herod is going to search for the child to kill him." So he got up, took the child and his mother during the night and left for Egypt, where he stayed until the death of Herod. And so was fulfilled what the Lord had said through the prophet: "Out of Egypt I called my son."

As we know from that famous Scripture, He is our Shepherd, and He will lead us through the valley of the shadow of death.

His rod and staff will comfort us. Goodness and mercy shall follow us all the days of our lives.

God is that good Shepherd, so anytime we want guidance – just key the co-ordinates into God and His guidance system will kick into operation.

GOD HAS HIS OWN GUIDING SYSTEM IN THE FORM OF THE HOLY SPIRIT AND ANGELS.

SECURITY COUNCIL

The security council of the United Nations (UN) is made up of the five most powerful nations in the world – namely United States, Russia, China, France and the United Kingdom. You would have thought that with these countries on board – evil would cease to spread it's tentacles of violence, destruction and terror on a global basis.

This is not the case as countries are taking personal measures to ensure that they are insulated from the potential dangers that can arise. Countries are even ignoring the advice of the UN Security Councils as we can see "veto power" being used to overrule decisions made by the UN.

In early 2006, Israel made a pre-emptive strike on Lebanon despite the UN's advice. The reason for what some may term a blatant disregard for authority can be linked to Israel's motive for war – Israel are fighting for their survival as a nation while other nations may be fighting for "other precious commodities".

In Psalm 91, we are advised of the most powerful Security Council that guarantees our survival for a very long time. Below is a subset of the security that you will receive:

You will not fear the terror of night, nor the arrow that flies by day, nor the pestilence that stalks in the darkness, nor the plague that destroys at midday. A thousand may fall at your side, ten thousand at your right hand, but it

will not come near you. You will only observe with your eyes and see the punishment of the wicked.

So let us shore up our defenses by dwelling in the secret place of the Most High.

SHOCK AND AWE

As Christians we sometimes forget that, just as God is merciful, He can also be 'terrible' when His decrees are ignored. His acts can be so terrible that the opposition has no choice but to succumb.

In 2003, Saddam Hussein was advised by the United Nations to get rid of his country's alleged stockpile of WMD (or Weapons of Mass Destruction). The advice was ignored and the full might of the United States Armed forces was unleashed, resulting in the term 'shock and awe'.

Pharaoh was advised by Moses to set the Israelites free so they could worship God in the desert. Just as Saddam ignored advice and was subjected to a massive onslaught, Pharaoh ignored plenty of advice given by the LORD and experienced 'shock and awe' tactics of a different nature and level, and in the end he had no choice but to let the people go. Exodus 13 v 14 – 16 gives us an insight into this nature of God:

"In days to come, when your son asks you, 'What does this mean?' say to him, 'With a mighty hand the LORD brought us out of Egypt, out of the land of slavery.

When Pharaoh stubbornly refused to let us go, the LORD killed every firstborn in Egypt, both man and animal. This is why I sacrifice to the LORD the first male offspring of every womb and redeem each of my first born sons.'

And it will be like a sign on your hand and a symbol on your forehead that the LORD brought us out of Egypt with his mighty hand."

LORD we ask for the grace to obey Your every decree, so we do not experience your 'terrible' nature.

SHOW ME THE MONEY

Little did Cuba Gooding Jr. know how much this statement he made in the course of his Oscar-winning performance in the film Jerry Maguire would impact our lives!

Money is one of the most controversial issues faced by the church in terms of scandals, lack of integrity and authenticity behind the claim that God demands specific amounts in the form of tithes or offerings.

A tithe pretty much speaks for itself – a tenth of your income. The amount to donate as an offering is not clear cut, as we sometimes see from the questionable formulae presented at some church meetings.

Should we be bothered?

My answer is two-fold. 'Yes', in terms of the ability to lead people astray, and 'No' based on the response given to my spirit by the Mighty Counsellor.

If I gave out of my lack and the LORD guarantees me long life and prosperity, surely this is much better than not giving out of my abundance and facing a sickness that will wipe away the abundance?

MONEY IS THE ONE OF THE MOST CONTROVERSIAL ISSUES FACED BY THE CHURCH IN TERMS OF SCANDALS

Offerings should be a form of worship to the Lord Almighty. So rather than trying to figure out the gymnastics of giving, we should give with a faithful heart. The next time we hear the Scripture below from Malachi 3 verses 8 - 12 quoted when it is time to give an offering, we should rejoice and thank God for all He has done in our lives -:

"Will a man rob God? Yet you rob me, "But you ask, 'How do we rob you? "In tithes and offerings. You are under a curse - the whole nation of you - because you are robbing me. Bring the whole tithe into the storehouse, that there may be food in my house. Test me in this," says the LORD Almighty, "and see if I will not throw open the floodgates of heaven and pour out so much blessing that you will not have room enough for it. I will prevent pests from devouring your crops, and the vines in your fields will not cast their fruit," says the LORD Almighty. "Then all the nations will call you blessed, for yours will be a delightful land," says the LORD Almighty.

It is the heart behind the giving that the LORD treasures most!

STAND AND DELIVER

I have always questioned myself about reaching heaven and finding out that I have missed God's plan for my life. Life starts and then it ends with death. It is so short that we will need God's help to ensure that we are on the right track.

In our lifetime, we will encounter different kinds of people along the track – rich, poor, great, proud, humble, selfish, kind, blessed, sick, healthy, masters, servants etc but when all is said and done, it is the judgment of God and not people which is the final "leveller"

On that final day of judgment will we be able to stand or will we hide in fear as highlighted in Revelations 6 v 14 – 17:

The sky receded like a scroll, rolling up, and every mountain and island was removed from its place. Then the kings of the earth, the princes, the generals, the rich, the mighty, and every slave and every free man hid in caves and among the rocks of the mountains. They called to the mountains and the rocks, "Fall on us and hide us from the face of Him who sits on the throne and from the wrath of the Lamb! For the great day of their wrath has come, and who can stand?"

We need to do everything by the grace of God to stand tall and be worthy on the day of judgment.

SYSTEM DEMO

The scene is set – the marketing representative and his assistant go through their final preparation for what could make or break their company. This account is crucial for the injection of cash for the future survival of the company. Sweats of nerves can be seen on the face of the assistant as he paces up and down the conference room.

The scene is the demonstration of the firm's latest offering to facilitate cash flow accounting throughout the client's global organisation. The approval of the account is dependent on the outcome of the system demonstration. Key decision makers and influencers will be present and their "nod" is crucial to the final approval.

No organisation will approve the expenditure of millions without evidence of the value that will be obtained. There needs to be convincing evidence that will influence this key decision. As the age old adage goes - "Actions speak louder than Words. We see an example highlighted in 1 Kings 18 v 34 – 39:

Do it again," he said, and they did it again. Do it a third time," he ordered, and they did it the third time. The water ran down around the altar and even filled the trench. At the time of sacrifice, the prophet Elijah stepped forward and prayed: "O LORD, God of Abraham, Isaac and Israel, let it be known today that you are God in Israel and that I am your servant and have done all these things at your command. Answer me, O LORD; answer me, so these people will know that you, O LORD, are God, and that you are turning their hearts back again. Then the fire of the LORD fell and burned up the sacrifice, the wood, the stones and the soil, and also licked up the water in the trench. When all the people saw this, they fell prostrate and cried, "The LORD He is God! The LORD -He is God!

TEACHER TEACHER

The lucrative rewards from professional public speaking cannot be underestimated, as we see the flurry of posters advertising yet another conference, seminar, or public gathering.

Everyone now wants to be involved in the art of giving advice and tips on the latest fad, which can range from sports and motivational tips, to religion and the Word of God. In my opinion, some of these speaking engagements can be a waste of time if they have no impact in terms of value creation.

Acquiring the knowledge and discipline to be a teacher takes time. The process of maturity is facilitated over a certain period and when it happens people will flock to you, as was evident in the visit of the Queen of Sheba to King Solomon.

The impact of effective teaching can be seen in Luke 4 verse 36 – 37, as Jesus demonstrated His mastery and skill in the art of delivery:

All the people were amazed and said to each other, "What is this teaching? With authority and power He gives orders to evil spirits and they come out!" And the news about Him spread throughout the surrounding area.

Your gift will make way for you as you make an impact in the lives of people by effective teaching that demonstrates authority and power.

THE BOLD AND THE BEAUTIFUL

One can only be amazed on one hand, and sad on the other at the utter boldness with which terrorists carry out their deadly missions.

Death is not a discouraging factor, since they believe they have been promised riches of another kind in a 'paradise' defined by their leaders. This makes them ready to do anything to sway the policies of countries that do not share their beliefs. Year after year, innocent people are subjected to periods of mourning as their loved ones fall victim to terrorist attacks whose perpetrators seek to force realignment with their beliefs.

As Christians, we have a faith which gives every individual the freedom to choose to worship and glorify a beautiful God. That freedom of choice is currently being challenged by government policies that will restrict the teaching of the gospel. Do we sit down and keep quiet, or should we let the government know our convictions, as Peter made clear to the rulers and elders of the land in Acts 4 v 16 – 20:

"What are we going to do with these men?" they asked. "Everybody living in Jerusalem knows they have done an outstanding miracle, and we cannot deny it. But to stop this thing from spreading any further among the people, we must warn these men to speak no longer to anyone in this name."

Then they called them in again and commanded them not to speak or teach at all in the name of Jesus. But Peter and John replied, "Judge for yourselves whether it is right in God's sight to obey you rather than God. For we cannot help speaking about what we have seen and heard."

As one Pastor pointed out, we need to stand up and be counted by adopting strategies that our God will lay on a gold platter when we seek His counsel.

Whatever happens, remember He is in control, and we should allow 'the Grandmaster' to move all the pieces of the puzzle into the right place by yielding to His instructions.

THE GIFT AND THE GIVER

In my opinion there is a fine line between honouring and worshipping our leaders. This is more apparent in the African culture as we are brought up to respect and "fear" our elders. Hence when we make introductions or acknowledge the presence of a speaker, it is sometimes with a lot of awe coupled with some "fear and trembling" to the detriment of sometimes neglecting the "The Giver" of the gift.

This fine line can also present a hindrance when circumstances warrant the confrontation of a leader who has not done the right thing. There are perfect examples of organisations that have since "bitten the dust" as the fear of confrontation has been a stumbling block to performing due diligence on their operations.

Revelation 19 v 9 – 10, highlights a similar scenario and the response given by the one who possessed the gift:

Then the angel said to me, "Write: 'Blessed are those who are invited to the wedding supper of the Lamb!' "And he added, "These are the true words of God." At this I fell at his feet to worship him. But he said to me, "Do not do it! I am a fellow servant with you and with your brothers

who hold to the testimony of Jesus. Worship God! For the testimony of Jesus is the spirit of prophecy."

The Giver of everything is God and we pray for the grace not to forget to acknowledge Him in all things.

THE KINGMAKER

Politics is a very interesting game as opponents try every trick in the book to get elected into office for either a first term or to extend their current tenure. The trickery does not just happen between opposing parties but it even rears its ugly head in the selection of candidates to run for office within the same party.

In this game there is a group of people known as the Kingmakers who just sit back and influence the selection of a candidate for these positions. They are not interested in running but derive their satisfaction from exerting their power of influence.

As Christians we have a Kingmaker who has guaranteed our selection into heaven as highlighted in Revelation 5 v 9 - 10:

And they sang a new song, saying: " You are worthy to take the scroll, And to open its seals; For You were slain, And have redeemed us to God by Your blood Out of every tribe and tongue and people and nation, And have made us kings and priests to our God; And we shall reign on the earth."

Jesus is the ultimate kingmaker who is worthy and has received power, riches, wisdom, strength, honor, glory and blessings from the power base up in the heavenly realms.

THE LITMUS TEST

In my opinion, the proliferation of churches, televangelists, and conferences has provided opportunity for a lot of spiritual abuse due to diverse interpretations.

I have often questioned the concept of the 'laying upon of hands'; not of its undeniable benefits with regards healing, but the perception that its effectiveness depends on the number of people that fall down under the anointing. Surely, it is the power of the anointing that causes one to fall, not how hard you 'lay your hands', or how many people you can touch in a specific time frame.

This leaves us with the dilemma of how to test the authenticity of spiritual truths transmitted over the airwaves of society. There are two litmus tests which can be found in 1 John 4 v 1 - 3 and 1 John 4 v 6 that can guide us in discerning the truth:

Dear friends, do not believe every spirit, but test the spirits to see whether they are from God, because many false prophets have gone out into the world.

This is how you can recognise the Spirit of God: Every spirit that acknowledges that Jesus Christ has come in

the flesh is from God, but every spirit that does notacknowledge Jesus is not from God. This is the spirit of the antichrist, which you have heard is coming and even now is already in the world.

We are from God, and whoever knows God listens to us; but whoever is not from God does not listen to us. This is how we recognize the Spirit of truth and the spirit of falsehood.

THE POWER OF ONE

One should not underestimate the impact an individual can have on the world.

Martin Luther King, Mother Teresa, Adolf Hitler, John Wesley, Gandhi. I could name several individuals who have impacted society in both good and bad ways.

It is so easy to give excuses; that the tasks are too big or we do not have the resources to carry out an assignment for God. God is just looking for one person who will be faithful and committed to putting His plans on earth into action.

The power of one - whether good or bad - is confirmed in Romans 5 v 18 -19:

Yes, Adam's one sin brought condemnation upon everyone, but Christ's one act of righteousness makes all people right in God's sight and gives them life. Because one person disobeyed God, many people became sinners. But because one other person obeyed God, many people will be made right in God's sight.

Through one person sin entered the world, and through one Person all sins have been forgiven. I pray that God will give each of us the grace to be relevant in our own little way.

THE STRUGGLES OF LIFE

Do you ever wonder why we struggle in those three areas of life commonly associated with sin – the lust of the flesh, the lust of the eyes and the pride of life - considering that the Word tells us that God's grace is sufficient?

If it is sufficient, why do we still desperately struggle in all these areas?

God, in His awesome manner, gave me an insight into the potential causes of our struggles. James 4 v 5 – 8 highlights the following:

Or do you think Scripture says without reason that the spirit he caused to live in us envies intensely?

But he gives us more grace. That is why Scripture says: "God opposes the proud but gives grace to the humble.

Submit yourselves, then to God. Resist the devil and he will flee from you.

Come near to God and he will come near to you. Wash your hands, you sinners, and purify your hearts, you double - minded.

Do my struggles with lust and pride then mean that I do not have the grace necessary to eliminate them?

This may not be the case, but it seems that some of the actions we have to implement to receive grace are as follows:

- Resist the devil
- Humble ourselves
- Purify our hearts and wash our hands.

I guess we need to take a serious look inwards with the help of the Holy Spirit to implement these, to enable us repent and get the grace we so desperately need.

THERE CAN BE MIRACLES – IF YOU BELIEVE!

The title of a bestselling song, but the question is still relevant today.

God will do a miracle in your life today - 'AMEN!' is the echo that we are so used to hearing, conference after conference. The question that comes to mind is, do we really believe in miracles or are our answers just another automatic response to a Christian cliché?

If an angel appeared to us right now, how would we react to the message of good tidings that he would bring? In my opinion, it is the grace of God that facilitates our response, because if you have never had the privilege of being exposed to the wonderful phenomenon that is God, it is hard to tell how you would react, and whether you would accept the authenticity of such news.

In the two Scriptures below, we see the reaction of two different individuals.

Luke 1 v 18 - 20 gives details of the first response:

Zechariah asked the angel, "How can I be sure of this? I am an old man and my wife is well along in years."

The angel answered, "I am Gabriel. I stand in the presence of God, and I have been sent to speak to you and to tell you this good news. And now you will be silent and not able to speak until the day this happens, because you did not believe my words, which will come true at their proper time."

Further in v 34 – 38 we see a different response:

"How will this be," Mary asked the angel, "since I am a virgin?" The angel answered, "The Holy Spirit will come

upon you, and the power of the Most High will overshadow you. So the holy one to be born will be called the Son of God.

Even Elizabeth your relative is going to have a child in her old age, and she who was said to be barren is in her sixth month.

For nothing is impossible with God.

"I am the Lord's servant," Mary answered. "May it be to me as you have said." Then the angel left her.

I would have expected Zechariah – 'a true man of God' according to the description of his lifestyle in the Scriptures - to have believed that with God, nothing is impossible. It was Mary's response - an innocent virgin - that highlights the attitude to adopt in believing in the possibility of a miracle: *'May it be as you have said!'*

We just need to believe with childlike faith that with God all things are possible, and we should not try to figure out how it will be accomplished.

THEY THINK IT'S ALL OVER!

If you have not yet experienced God's different battle approaches, it would be easy to think that the victory belongs to the adversary.

Some years ago, the Japanese introduced a manufacturing method called 'Just in Time', which eliminates the need for excess storage. Goods were manufactured in response to orders and not based on forecasts, thereby eliminating excess capacity.

God is a 'Just in Time' being. He is never late, and He carries out His plans according to His schedule, not man's.

The waiting period that God subjects us to during battle is to develop our character, patience and trust in Him. Hence we remember the lyrics of a popular gospel song that says, *'Late in the midnight hour, God's gonna turn it around...and around and around.'*

As I write this, the government has allowed the Racial and Religious Hatred Bill to pass through the House of Commons en route to the House of Lords, where it could eventually be made law. This is a bill that is designed to prevent the name of the LORD from being glorified.

To those who do not understand the ways of God it may seem like it is all over, but as the kingdom of darkness found out in 1 Corinthians 2 verses 7 – 9, it is only over when God, the Alpha and Omega, says so:

No, we speak of God's secret wisdom, a wisdom that has been hidden and that God destined for our glory before

time began. None of the rulers of this age understood it, for if they had, they would not have crucified the Lord of glory.

However, as it is written: "No eye has seen, no ear has heard, no mind has conceived what God has prepared for those who love him."

TRUST ME!

There is a famous fable about the chicken that was cooking a delicious meal, and it needed assistance to collect ingredients.

All the animals in the farm were asked to help, but all gave the same response: 'We are busy.' The chicken went through all the laborious tasks alone, and when the meal was ready it threw open another invitation. 'Would you lovely animals like to join me in eating this delicious meal?'

Without any hesitation, each one of the animals replied, 'YES PLEASE!'

It is amazing how easy it is to exhibit faithfulness during good times. A few challenges and difficulties can show how faithful we really are. The dangers of relying on unfaithful people - like those 'busy' animals that were only interested in lining their stomachs with the delicacies - can be seen in Proverbs 25 v 19:

Like a bad tooth or a lame foot is reliance on the unfaithful in times of trouble.

This principle is very important for the process of team selection and building. We need to select people who will be in for the long haul.

The football industry is not a good example of this, as we see players jumping ship when their clubs get relegated, since money is the main motivator.

UNTIL DEATH DO US PART!

I am currently fasting with the rest of my church for the salvation of souls in London.

To say that I am struggling is an understatement, as my flesh constantly wants to be fed and sulks like a baby if it does not get its way!

The sermon delivered last Sunday challenged me about the level of commitment we must possess when working for God. How desperately do we want to be used by God? An important point highlighted was that affection for the things of God is a major driver and catalyst, which motivates our obedience and diligence.

During a fast, we need to understand the objective, and ask God for a 'die hard' level of grace to complete the given task. This is highlighted in Job 13 v 14 - 15:

Why do I put myself in jeopardy and take my life in my hands?

Though He slay me, yet will I hope in Him; I will surely defend my ways to His face.

When you have a genuine affection for someone or something, it makes the tasks much easier to perform, and reduces the struggles. May God provide us with the grace to be affectionate, passionate and diligent for His things.

It is not surprising that most of us are willing to do anything for our loved ones during that passionate period of courting! No mountain is too high to climb and no distance too far to walk!

VISION IMPOSSIBLE

As a leader, it can be frustrating when those you are leading do not plug into what you believe to be a godly vision.

It is even more disheartening when you are a hundred percent sure, but the main resistance comes from those you believe should understand and run with the vision. I am not suggesting that everyone is supposed to catch the vision, but Acts 7 v 25 – 29 prompts leaders to ask the following questions:

1. Have we communicated the vision accurately?
2 Do the people really understand the vision, and how they are supposed to complement it?

Moses thought that his own people would realize that God was using him to rescue them, but they did not. The next day Moses came upon two Israelites who were fighting. He tried to reconcile them by saying, 'Men, you are brothers; why do you want to hurt each other?' "But the man who was mistreating the other pushed Moses aside and said, 'Who made you ruler and judge over us? Do you want to kill me as you killed the Egyptian yesterday?' When Moses heard this, he fled to Midian, where he settled as a foreigner and had two sons."

Later in Acts 7 v 33 – 34, the burning bush experience with God facilitates a greater understanding of the vision that God had for the children of Israel and Moses' role in leading them out of Egypt.

"Then the Lord said to him, 'Take off your sandals; the place where you are standing is holy ground.

I have indeed seen the oppression of my people in Egypt. I have heard their groaning and have come down to set them free. Now come, I will send you back to Egypt.

For people to run with a vision, they need to have greater knowledge, understanding and wisdom of it, and of what their roles are.

WAR COLLEGE

On the 11th January 1879, a five thousand strong British Army under the leadership of Lord Chelmsford invaded Zululand to keep the region unified under British Rule. If only one had read the scripture to him which highlights that "it is not by might or power but by the spirit says the Lord".

His confidence in the British war machine was so strong that he showed little respect for the fighting qualities of the Zulus. He was known to quote the following:

"If I am called upon to conduct operations against them,' he wrote in July 1878, I shall strive to be in a position to show them how hopelessly inferior they are to us in fighting power, although' numerically stronger"

This dangerous mixture of self-confidence and contempt for their foes infected the whole British force. But their misjudgement came to rebound on them badly as the culmination of Chelmsford's incompetence was a blood-soaked field littered with thousands of corpses. Of the original 1,750 defenders - 1,000 British and 750 black auxiliaries - 1,350 had been killed.

Please note that the Zulu commander did not even attend any of the top notch "war colleges" yet caused so much havoc that the British public was dumbstruck by the news that 'spear-wielding savages' had defeated the well equipped British Army.

The story above is a reminder that as Christians, the effective weapons that guarantee victory are not flesh and blood but weapons of a more spiritual nature as highlighted in 2 Corinthians 10 v 3 – 6:

For though we live in the world, we do not wage war as the world does. The weapons we fight with are not the weapons of the world. On the contrary, they have divine power to demolish strongholds. We demolish arguments and every pretension that sets itself up against the knowledge of God, and we take captive every thought to make it obedient to Christ. And we will be ready to punish every act of disobedience, once your obedience is complete.

WHERE THERE'S A WILL...

We all know the phrase that says, 'Where there's a will, there's a way.'

In other words, if we are motivated enough we will find a way to achieve any task. Money, promotion, status, recognition, titles, tangible and intangible rewards are some of the things that incentivise us and give us the willpower to accomplish even the most difficult tasks.

In writing about this, I began to think that some of the tasks we accomplish may not necessarily be God's will for us, despite the reward and recognition that we gain.

So, how do we know the will of God?

1 Thessalonians 4 verses 3 – 8 confirms that our starting point is God's words as laid out in Scripture, concept upon concept and principle upon principle.

Rest assured, obedience to the Word of God is the starting point as we seek His perfect will for our lives:

It is God's will that you should be sanctified: that you should avoid sexual immorality;
that each of you should learn to control his own body in a way that is holy and honourable, not in passionate lust like the heathen, who do not know God;
and that in this matter no one should wrong his brother or take advantage of him. The Lord will punish men for all such sins, as we have already told you and warned you.

For God did not call us to be impure, but to live a holy life.

Therefore, he who rejects this instruction does not reject man but God, who gives you his Holy Spirit.

Where there's God's will, there is God's way!

PART 2

RELATIONSHIP
WITH SELF

YOU FORGOT MY 'TITLE'

Bishop, Pastor, Deacon, Director, Engineer, Apostle, Lawyer, and Architect, to name a few, are titles given to individuals based on their profession.

From country to country, there are differences in determining whether certain titles are legitimate or self-imposed.

The dictionary defines 'title' as follows:

A formal appellation attached to the name of a person or family by virtue of office, rank, hereditary privilege, noble birth, or attainment or used as a mark of respect.

Question: Is this the case with most of the titles defined in society; can they be associated with respect?

I leave the answer to you, but will contribute my bit by highlighting that the word "title" is a descriptive word that does not define the character of the individual to which it is attached.

The Bible, in Matthew 7 v 16, gives us an insight into why a title is not sufficient to describe an individual:

"You will fully recognise them by their fruits. Do people pick grapes from thorns, or figs from thistles?"

We should focus on developing our character to define who we are, and not lose sleep about whether we are addressed by our titles or not.

ANOINTED FOR THE NEW YEAR

Regardless of religion, New Year's Eve is one of the most celebrated events throughout the world.

It is a time for reflection – depending on your state - as the clock strikes twelve and we hug and kiss each other, thanking God for ushering us into the New Year.

Resolutions are made, only to be broken within the first couple of weeks. Health clubs and gyms are 'wise as serpents' as they insert twelve-month minimum membership clauses into their joining contracts. They know that the volume of applications increases in January, only for them to get cancellation requests weeks later as the reality of the commitment and dedication required sets in.

As we reflect on the past and coming years, let us remind ourselves of the dedication, commitment and enablement that comes from God alone as we derive our resolutions, mission statements or life statements. Luke 4 verse 18 – 19 gives us the perfect template:

"The Spirit of the Lord is on me, because He has anointed me to preach good news to the poor. He has sent me to proclaim freedom for the prisoners and recovery of sight for the blind, to release the oppressed, to proclaim the year of the Lord's favour."

This template enables us to have something to reflect on at the end of the year. It will give us purpose and meaning as we live, remembering that each day the LORD gives us is a gift, and that we must redeem the time and maximize every moment.

ARISE AND SHINE

As the pastor announces yet another period of prayer and fasting, a couple of sad faces begin to form - including yours truly!

The subject is not on the bestselling shelf of my little library!

I know that the LORD encourages that certain things only go out by prayer and fasting, but we need to move to the next level after carrying out such spiritual exercises. Some churches will earn 'Oscars' for the amount of prayer and fasting they undertake, but can they truly reflect what is highlighted in 1 Corinthians 4 v 20 ?

For the kingdom of God is not a matter of talk but of power.

Do not get me wrong, prayer and fasting is good and necessary. But so is acting to reflect that God has already guaranteed the victory.

Our daily lives need to reflect God's power working within us and we must live the kingdom of God, not just talk about it. Praying and fasting is part of the process of achieving this goal.

BOYZ II MEN

A strict ceremony most Jewish boys have to go through is the bar mitzvah, which marks their passage from boyhood to manhood.

Different cultures have various ways of celebrating this phase in a boy's life. In Swaziland, I hear that a lion has to be killed with bare hands to confirm manhood!

Regardless of the details of the ceremony, the passage comes with changes in the way a man conducts his affairs. I hear that during the bar mitzvah, elders give advice on different subjects, ranging from money management to the treatment of other people preparing him for what he will face in future.

The Bible confirms the importance of this phase and what it entails in 1 Corinthians 13 v 11 – 12:

When I was a child, I talked like a child; I thought like a child, I reasoned like a child. When I became a man, I put childish ways behind me.

Now we see but a poor reflection as in a mirror; then we shall see face to face. Now I know in part; then I shall know fully, even as I am fully known.

There is a time in our lives when we need to grow up and move from drinking milk to eating meat. We have the added advantage of having the Holy Spirit with us every step of the way.

CHAIN REACTION

A nuclear bomb is set off by an atom disintegrating to set off a chain reaction, which initiates the massive explosion experienced with a nuclear blast.

The damage and impact caused by the fission of the initial atom in the explosion generates the energy and inertia which leads to the final blast.

Quite amazing, the impact of a single atom!

Just as one atom can cause a nuclear chain reaction, an individual can cause a chain reaction in the spreading of the Gospel by his actions. In Philippians 1 v 12 - 14, we see the impact Paul's imprisonment had among the palace guards as he used his status to spread the Gospel:

Now I want you to know, brothers, that what has happened to me has really served to advance the gospel.

As a result, it has become clear throughout the whole palace guard and to everyone else that I am in chains for Christ.

Because of my chains, most of the brothers in the Lord have been encouraged to speak the word of God more courageously and fearlessly.

We should not underestimate the impact that our actions have when it comes to spreading the Gospel. Twelve men under the tutelage of Jesus Christ initiated the explosion of the Gospel, and the impact grows from day to day. All our actions are relevant when it comes to carrying out the work of God.

COLOUR BLIND

'I will call you tomorrow', 'Tell them I am not in', 'Let's do lunch', 'The cheque is in the post', 'Did you get my messages?', 'Did you check your answering machine?' - only to find out later that the person does not have one or did not switch it on!

I could go on, but these are examples of words we utter, not with the intention of harming anyone, but as excuses to justify our actions.

'Our mother told us to tell you that she is not in - Goodbye!

'In its attempt to justify everything, the world classifies some lies as 'white', but as Christians we have no choice but to speak the only kind of truth - the real truth. In situations where we have lied and entrapped ourselves, we are advised in Proverbs 6 v 2 - 5 of the perfect remedy:

If you have been trapped by what you said, ensnared by the words of your mouth, Then do this, my son, to free yourself, since you have fallen into your neighbour's hands: Go and humble yourself; press your plea with your neighbour!

Allow no sleep to your eyes, no slumber to your eyelids. Free yourself, like a gazelle from the hand of the hunter, like a bird from the snare of the fowler.

COMPETITIVE ADVANTAGE

What is the difference between the services/products provided by the following?

1. Microsoft versus Amstrad

2. Tesco versus Lidl

3. British Airways versus Easy Jet

They all provide the same products and services but there is something that distinguishes one from the other. This uniqueness is what organisations use to set themselves apart from others and as a marketing tool to attract customers. It is what gives organisations competitive advantage over their competitors.

My final question – What is the difference between a Christian and a Non Christian when you take into account the following:

1. Non Christians are involved in providing charitable services and in some cases are much more organized
2. Non Christians can be generous, friendly, kind and loving

In my opinion, the answer lies in our relationship with Jesus. This is what should give us that competitive advantage in every aspect of our lives. By having a relationship with Christ we can ask him what we need to do each day to have that advantage. We are advised in Proverbs 8 v 12 that the wisdom of God will give us insight into what we can do to get that edge:

I wisdom dwell with prudence, and find out knowledge of witty inventions

I particularly like the translation of "witty" by the American Heritage Dictionary which gives a "qualitative" meaning to one of the attributes of the wisdom of God:

Entertainingly and strikingly clever or original in concept, design, or performance

This concludes what we already know - that all things originated from the Almighty God.

DON'T BELIEVE THE HYPE

Pride is the most subtle of weapons used by the enemy, especially when it comes through the contributions of a third party.

Personal assistants to Hollywood stars go to extra lengths to get them on the right shows to remind the public how great their clients are.

At seminars and conferences, we are used to hearing the phrases 'great man of God', 'awesome man of God' and 'powerful man of God'. Inasmuch as this may be true, we must take care and remember that without God, we are nothing. In Him we live, move and have our being.

PRIDE IS THE MOST SUBTLE OF WEAPONS USED BY THE ENEMY

As we know, with the media one day you may be up there and the next you could be down, which in a way mirrors what the Bible says in Matthew 23 v 12:

"For whoever exalts himself will be humbled, and whoever humbles himself will be exalted."

ECONOMIC THEORY

Economics teaches us that in most situations, supply cannot meet the ever-increasing demands of man.

This causes an imbalance between supply and demand that results in either a deficit where demand outweighs supply, or on the other hand, a surplus where supply outweighs demand.

As a result, we need to learn to adjust to live within these constraints. Philippians 4 v 11 – 13 relates to this by advising us to be content in God, who is the supplier of all our needs and not wants!

I am not saying this because I am in need, for I have learned to be content whatever the circumstances.

I know what it is to be in need, and I know what it is to have plenty. I have learned the secret of being content in any and every situation, whether well fed or hungry, whether living in plenty or in want.

I can do everything through him who gives me strength.

As that famous song goes, 'In Him we live, move and have our being'.

EMPTY BARREL

At work a few years ago, there was a period when I could not get myself assigned on to a project.

When one finally came along, I had to leverage some knowledge from a senior manager to prepare for the role. To appear suitable for the job, instead of making clear that I was deficient in a particular subject, I gave a round of inaccurate answers thinking he would not notice the difference – WRONG!

In a polite and professional way, he pointed out that one of the things he disliked most was people trying to give a false impression of what they know. He pointed out that he would have preferred it if I had admitted my ignorance, so he could assist me in my area of weakness.

WE SOMETIMES THINK WE HAVE MANAGED TO TALK OUR WAY OUT OF SITUATIONS, JUST BECAUSE PEOPLE DO NOT SAY ANYTHING.

That lesson sticks in my mind to this day. We sometimes think we have managed to talk our way out of situations, just because people do not say anything. Rather than give excuses to make ourselves look good, we need to humble ourselves and ask what we can do to improve the situation, as highlighted in Luke 3 v 7 – 14:

John said to the crowds coming out to be baptized by him, "You brood of vipers! Who warned you to flee from the coming wrath?

Produce fruit in keeping with repentance. And do not begin to say to yourselves, 'We have Abraham as our father.' For I tell you that out of these stones God can raise up children for Abraham.

The axe is already at the root of the trees, and every tree that does not produce good fruit will be cut down and thrown into the fire."

"What should we do then?" the crowd asked.

John answered, "The man with two tunics should share with him who has none, and the one who has food should do the same."

Tax collectors also came to be baptized. "Teacher," they asked, "what should we do?"

"Don't collect any more than you are required to," he told them.

Then some soldiers asked him, "And what should we do?" He replied, "Don't extort money and don't accuse people falsely - be content with your pay."

ERROR LOG

Majority of projects compile what is called an "Error Log" during the testing phase as a mechanism to monitor the performance of the system. The log monitors the behaviour of the system under various tests so that decisions can be carried out on potential adjustments that are required under the different scenarios.

In Daniel 6 v 3 - 5, we see the attempt of the governors and satraps of Babylon to compile a type of "error log" against Daniel to undermine him in the presence of King Darius.

Then this Daniel distinguished himself above the governors and satraps, because an excellent spirit was in him; and the king gave thought to setting him over the whole realm. So the governors and satraps sought to find some charge against Daniel concerning the kingdom; but they could find no charge or fault, because he was faithful; nor was there any error or fault found in him. Then these men said, "We shall not find any charge against this Daniel unless we find it against him concerning the law of his God."

We are advised that the enemy prowls like a lion every single day in his role to find fault in us, but praise be to God that we are under no condemnation because of the blood of Jesus. Like Daniel, let us live a faithful life in the strength of Jesus Christ so that an "error log" is not compiled and used against us.

FANCY DRESS

Every parent knows that look on their children's faces as they give you the invitation to yet another "party of the year". As far as children are concerned, every party they are invited to is important and the logistics behind them must be adhered to with military precision.

When it comes to a fancy dress party, the logistical arrangement is of a different kind as you assume the role of an apprentice mini cab driver scouting the streets of London for the **"right"** costume. Based on experience you also pray that no one else wears the same costume at the party or else...... Let me put it in a humorous way – *Carry some additional clothing!*

The importance of putting on the "right" costume or dress for the "right" occasion can not be more overemphasised than in Ephesians 6 v 13 – 18 where we are advised that these elements of clothing have to be worn at all times:

Therefore put on the full armor of God, so that when the day of evil comes, you may be able to stand your ground, and after you have done everything, to stand. Stand firm then, with the belt of truth buckled around your waist, with the breastplate of righteousness in place, and with your feet fitted with the readiness that comes from the gospel of peace. In addition to all this, take up the shield of faith, with which you can extinguish all the flaming arrows of the evil one. Take the helmet of salvation and the sword of the Spirit, which is the word of God. And pray in the Spirit on all occasions with all kinds of prayers and requests. With this in mind, be alert and always keep on praying for all the saints.

Just to point out, this is not fancy dress but a **"survival dress"**

FOOTBALL "FOCUS"

Walking with God can be very interesting and confusing sometimes. The Word of God in many forms advocates that we need to worship God with all our body, soul and mind – in other words "Total Focus".

This can only be achieved by the grace of God as distractions will always present an obstacle in achieving this state of mind. Interestingly enough, the dictionary defines distraction as the following:

"that which distracts, divides the attention, prevents concentration".

Prepare your heart for this scenario: – You are one hundred percent sure that God has told you to be under the tutelage of a leader. The leader and his leadership team do not show any sign of support. This is rather confusing because you are thinking – but God you told me to be under his leadership and I am not getting any support but resistance - What do you do?

SURELY GOOD THINGS WILL COME TO THOSE WHO WAIT

A similar scenario was presented in 2 Kings 2 v 2 – 5 where on three occasions the focus of Elisha kept him on track to become the successor of Elijah.

The company of the prophets at Jericho went up to Elisha and asked him, "Do you know that the LORD is going to take your master from you today? Yes, I know," he replied, but do not speak of it. Then Elijah said to him, "Stay here; the LORD has sent me to the Jordan. And he replied, As surely as the LORD lives and as you live, I will not leave you." So the two of them walked on.

As the words of a famous advert advocates "Surely good things will come to those who wait".

FRENCH CUISINE

When I was in the University, there were times when we reverted to a system of eating called 100, 010 or 001. This means that you had food only once a day – either at breakfast, lunch or dinner. This system was sometimes adopted not out of choice but necessity due to lack of funds.

This reminiscence was brought about by me trying to understand why I struggle in the discipline of fasting. The Holy Spirit brought to my attention that I needed to understand the motive behind fasting. The system in the University which in a way can be compared to a "partial fast" was adhered to because of the lack of funds. I needed to ask myself: "Is not this the fast that I have chosen?" ie. What is the motive behind the fast ?

These were comforting words as I began my research into the motives behind fasting and digested the case study in Matthew 17 v 19 – 21:

Then the disciples came to Jesus privately and said, "Why could we not cast it out?" So Jesus said to them, "Because of your unbelief; for assuredly, I say to you, if you have faith as a mustard seed, you will say to this mountain, 'Move from here to there,' and it will move; and nothing will be impossible for you. However, this kind does not go out except by prayer and fasting."

Some benefits that can be attributed to the discipline of fasting are:

1. It demonstrate the mastery of man over appetite, which led to it's downfall in the Garden of Eden;
2. It humbles the soul before God;
3. It crucifies the appetite so as to give entire time to prayer;
4. Prayer needs fasting for its development and growth;
5. It facilitates the demonstration of power over demons.

GREATER IS HE

You are taking the children to school and suddenly, another driver cuts in front of you, and your thoughts towards him are certainly not of love, goodness or kindness!

In a discussion with your wife she suddenly says something which, in your mind, means that the sun and moon will definitely go down and rise again before you settle that argument!

You drive past a young girl, still in secondary school – who is smoking away, oblivious to the damaging effect on her health - not to mention the effect on the ozone layer. You begin to wish that her parents were in the same room with you, forgetting that at some point in the past you were in her position, possibly smoking something much stronger.

IF WE ARE CREATED IN GOD'S IMAGE, WHY DO WE STILL EXPERIENCE REBELLION, RAGE, HATRED AND OTHER NEGATIVE EMOTIONS?

If we are created in God's image, why do we still experience rebellion, rage, hatred and other negative emotions? As I was still trying to get over the brother who did a Michael Schumacher move on me, I began to ponder – surely we are not created to have these feelings towards one another?

My thoughts were politely interrupted by the Holy Spirit, who pointed me in the direction of 1 John 4 v 4:

You, dear children, are from God and have overcome them, because the one who is in you is greater than the one who is in the world.

The reason why we get these feelings is because our spirit which is greater, needs to come to the surface so we can act accordingly. Our spirit needs to conquer our fleshy feelings.

Fasting helps in this regard, since it kills the flesh and feeds our spirit, coupled with the renewal of our minds with the Word of God.

GUESS WHAT!

One thing certain in life is that we have to make decisions on a daily basis.

We are presented daily with information from various sources, and the decisions we make based on this information can have both short and long term consequences. Irrational and emotional reactions to information can be detrimental, especially if we do not validate its source, accuracy and authenticity.

How many times have we reacted to situations without getting the whole picture? Mrs. A was supposed to have said something about Mrs. B, as narrated by Mrs. C. Mrs. B gets all emotional and responds negatively to Mrs. A without confirming the validity of the claim.

Company A begins construction of a building without approval and confirmation of the scope from its stakeholders, on the assumption that 'we always get confirmation and approval' from this company.

Basing your decisions on hearsay is a dangerous concept and should be discouraged. The Bible gives us some sound advice in Proverbs 18 v15 and 17:

The heart of the discerning acquires knowledge; the ears of the wise seek it out. The first to present his case seems right, till another comes forward and questions him.

HOLLYWOOD OR HOLY WOOD

Amazing how God can use diverse means to minister the Gospel of good news to an audience.

Years ago, I watched a film called Hurricane starring the Oscar winning actor, Denzel Washington. It was about a prize fighter who was wrongly accused of murder and sent to prison for a very long time.

During his stay in the prison, he did everything to keep his sanity. He read books, trained in the gym and kept himself busy to maximise the time. For me, the highlights of the film were two statements he made to focus himself on the tasks ahead:

"Deny myself of everything to be different including the luxuries to achieve my goal of becoming a prize fighter".

This mirrors the same advice given in 1 Corinthians 9 v 24 - 27:

Do you not know that in a race all the runners run, but only one gets the prize? Run in such a way as to get the prize.

Everyone who competes in the games goes into strict training. They do it to get a crown that will not last; but we do it to get a crown that will last forever.

Therefore I do not run like a man running aimlessly; I do not fight like a man beating the air.

No, I beat my body and make it my slave so that after I have preached to others, I myself will not be disqualified for the prize.

"Hate put me in jail, love is gonna get me out"

Similar to the advice given in 1 John 4 v 18:

There is no fear in love. But perfect love drives out fear, because fear has to do with punishment. The one who fears is not made perfect in love.

Have you ever wondered why some of the best known ministers of God spent time in a prison of some sort? Solitude does have its benefits, in that it makes you focus on what really matters in life!

HOSTILE TAKEOVER

Some time ago, after a heated argument with my wife, I began to wonder why husbands are on the enemy's main hit list.

I consulted my Helper and asked Him how I should react. We know we are to love our wives, but sometimes it is difficult and frustrating! Below is a synopsis of my perceived response from the Holy Spirit.

When a company launches a hostile takeover bid for another company, the target company seeks a 'White Knight' to support the defence plan. In most cases, the Chief Executive Officer and senior management of the target company will not just sit down and allow the opposition to gain ground. It takes on the hostile company with whatever defence strategy is agreed between itself and the 'White Knight'. The battle is not internal within the firm, but occurs externally between the host and target companies.

Rather than battle with your wife, launch a defence and attack strategy through your 'White Knight', Jesus. Just as the Chief Executive Officer has to defend the company, you also have to defend your company, which includes your wife, children and yourself. The enemy wants to launch a hostile takeover of your family, but we have an all-powerful 'White Knight' – Jesus and the heavenly host of angels.

We are reminded of the enemy's intention in John 10 v 10:

The thief comes only to steal and kill and destroy; I have come that they may have life, and have it to the full.

We need to focus on the main enemy in our battle plans and defend with all our heart, body and soul with the support of our defence team – God the Father, Son and Holy Ghost.

JUDGE AND JURY

It was one of those days; my beloved said something that wound me up.

On my way to work, I began to think of things that did not fit into the categories of holy, pure and loving. To get myself back into the right frame of mind I began to pray in tongues, and five minutes into the session, a text message arrived with the words 'I am sorry'.

As always the enemy had alternative plans, and suggested I respond to the text with the retort 'For what?', as the urge not to forgive was still strong.

Just as I was about to reply, I felt the Holy Spirit reminding me of the Scripture that talks about the number of times we must forgive. Another in John 8 verse 15 – 16 reminded me about the fallacy of the world's way of judgment:

You judge by human standards; I pass judgment on no one.

But if I do judge, my decisions are right, because I am not alone. I stand with the Father, who sent me.

The lesson I learnt that day, was that we should not judge and decide on the method of apology, but should graciously accept it..

The praying in tongues proved rewarding and life-saving, as I arrived in the city of London safe and unaffected by three terrorist bombs that had exploded in the area earlier.

Praise be to the Almighty God!

LASTING IMPRESSION

I was involved in an experiment with my colleagues, to see if we could tell the type of car they drive, the newspapers they read and the number of years they had worked with the organisation just by looking at them.

As expected, not all the answers were correct. The aim of the experiment was to highlight the dangers of perception.

One part of the body which tends to give a clear indication of a person's nature is their mouth. Life and death, as they say, are in the power of the tongue, so what we say can leave a lasting impression. Our spoken response to a situation can serve as a rough indication of the type of person we are, as highlighted in John 4 v 17 - 19:

"I have no husband," she replied. Jesus said to her, "You are right when you say you have no husband.

The fact is, you have had five husbands, and the man you now have is not your husband. What you have just said is quite true."

"Sir," the woman said, "I can see that you are a prophet.

Our fathers worshiped on this mountain, but you Jews claim that the place where we must worship is in Jerusalem."

Amazingly, the lady was previously married to five different men, yet not one word of rebuke came from Jesus. To make matters worse, she was now involved with a man who was not her husband. His non-judgmental response made the lady perceive that He was a prophet.

When you talk, who do people perceive you are - kind, loving, hateful, or merciful?

LEADERSHIP CRISIS

Jim Collin's book called *"Good to Great"* stresses the importance of good leadership. One of the factors that lead to the demise of nations, organizations, churches etc is bad leadership. There are numerous examples that we can cite from the rise and fall of Enron to the rise and fall of famous church institutions.

The importance of leadership means that all organizations should have an effective strategy in place to transfer leadership to facilitate the concept of "a going concern" - to ensure the organization continues to excel at what it does best. General Electric under the leadership of Jack Welch had their current CEO under the radar as a potential successor for a long time. He was amongst the Directors in GE that participated in the GE succession program.

In 1 Kings 19 v 15 – 16, we see the administering of God's succession strategy when it was apparent that the "post of prophet" had to be replaced as a result of Elijah's answer to God's question "what are you doing here"? in v 9 and 13 reflecting his discouragement.

The LORD said to him, "Go back the way you came, and go to the Desert of Damascus. When you get there, anoint Hazael king over Aram. Also, anoint Jehu son of Nimshi king over Israel, and anoint Elisha son of Shaphat from Abel Meholah to succeed you as prophet. Jehu will put to death any who escape the sword of Hazael, and Elisha will put to death any who escape the sword of Jehu."

God is never short of a replacement or successor as He confirms in v 18:

Yet I reserve seven thousand in Israel—all whose knees have not bowed down to Baal and all whose mouths have not kissed him."

LIAR LIAR

There was a time in the City of London when your "word was your bond". A gentleman's agreement was sealed by a handshake. Overnight we have seen the rapid increase in lawyers' fees as a lucrative market has been made in the drafting and reviewing of contract documentation.

Trust has gone out of the window and your potential saviour is your lawyer's ability to draft a "water-tight" contract which covers every potential fatality. The quality and contents of the contract document is so crucial that the wrong "ditto" and "phrase" can spell the loss of millions to a company during legal proceedings.

As usual the lawyers on both sides stand to lose nothing as they are rewarded for drafting the documents and also for appearing in court on your behalf. It is even amazing that contracts are drawn up between churches as the level of trust within the church seems to be dwindling.

THERE WAS A TIME IN THE CITY
OF LONDON WHEN YOUR
"WORD WAS YOUR BOND".
A GENTLEMAN'S AGREEMENT WAS
SEALED BY A HANDSHAKE.

I believe we need to take a leaf from Hebrews 6 v 16 – 18 on the area of trust:

Men swear by someone greater than themselves, and the oath confirms what is said and puts an end to all argument. Because God wanted to make the unchanging nature of His purpose very clear to the heirs of what was promised, he confirmed it with an oath. God did this so that, by two unchangeable things in which it is impossible for God to lie, we who have fled to take hold of the hope offered to us may be greatly encouraged.

LITTLE AND LARGE

Years ago, one of the most quoted prayers was the prayer of Jabez.

Part of this prayer got me thinking, as I watched the inauguration of the new Pope Benedict XVI on television. For some reason, I got judgemental as I criticised the religious procession and ceremony which accompanied the announcement.

The Holy Spirit - in His suave way - highlighted the fact that the appointment of this Pope and those before him had been allowed by God for a divine purpose. The best I could do was to seek God's counsel rather than complain - ouch! right below the belt!

This is how the issue of the prayer of Jabez in 1 Chronicles 4 v 10 came to light:

Jabez cried out to the God of Israel, "Oh, that you would bless me and enlarge my territory! Let your hand be with me and keep me from harm so that I will be free from pain." And God granted his request.

I do not know if I was free from pain as a result of the rebuke, but the Holy Spirit did a good job of expanding my territory in terms of my way of thinking. Enlarging our territory will involve expanding our scope of thinking beyond its current position.

MIND CONTROL

The long term consequences of anger are reflected in the following passages taken from Jonathan Aitken's account in his book "Pride and Perjury"

"After I read the Guardian articles in Switzerland .... This made my mood even more incendiary. So after a sleepless night (never the best background for good judgement) I made the decision to defend myself with an attack."

"In that dispirited but angry state of mind I sat down, without consulting anyone, to write my letter of resignation to the Prime Minister."

To be angry is to allow our mind to be in a dangerous and unstable state. This does not facilitate effective decision making as there is no solid foundation to make the right choice. The fact that God has given us the freedom of choice is not a license to make bad decision but an incentive to seek counsel to make the right decision.

1 Kings 20 v 11 – 12 highlights an example of a leader making a decision in a drunken and angry state of mind:

"So the king of Israel answered and said, "Tell him, 'Let not the one who puts on his armor boast like the one who takes it off.' And it happened when Ben-Hadad heard this message, as he and the kings were drinking at the command post, that he said to his servants, "Get ready." And they got ready to attack the city. "

TO BE ANGRY IS TO ALLOW OUR MIND TO BE IN A DANGEROUS AND UNSTABLE STATE.

Later in 1 Kings 20 v 21 we see the consequences of making decisions – unprepared, angry and in an unbalanced state of mind:

"Then the king of Israel went out and attacked the horses and chariots, and killed the Syrians with a great slaughter."

NO SMOKING POLICY

During a lunch break, I walked into a retail store to buy some stamps for a colleague.

At the stand, there was a captivating statement in big bold letters on the package of a product. The statement read – SMOKING KILLS!

Back in the day, I did my fair share of polluting the environment, and I began to wonder why we use our money to purchase a 'killer' product. No one wants to die, but why purchase a product that will aid and abet that process?

Romans 7 v 21 – 25 gives us possible insight into why sin, just like smoking, can be addictive and lead to death. We know it is bad, yet we sometimes blatantly commit the sinful act:

So I find this law at work: When I want to do good, evil is right there with me. For in my inner being I delight in God's law; but I see another law at work in the members of my body, waging war against the law of my mind and making me a prisoner of the law of sin at work within my members. What a wretched man I am! Who will rescue me from this body of death?
Thanks be to God—through Jesus Christ our Lord! So then, I myself in my mind am a slave to God's law, but in the sinful nature a slave to the law of sin.

As we can see, the power of addiction and bondage should not be underestimated. Even when warning signs are given to us through notices, the Word of God and so on, we still tend to ignore them.

Please LORD, give us the grace to avoid the pitfalls of death in our lives by obeying your Word.

NOT WHAT I SAY BUT WHAT I DO

How many times have we told our children not to do something, only for us to turn around and do the same thing?

'Stop shouting', 'Remember to say your prayers', 'Don't talk with your mouth full' are examples of such things. Children are unique in that they imitate what they see others do, especially their parents.

So, when you tell your children to tell someone on the phone that you are not in, the message they will deliver is 'Mummy told us to tell you that she is not in.' As far as they are concerned, Mummy is saying she is not in, but we know she is!

Children are more into the 'doing', rather than the 'saying'. The importance of leading by example for our children to imitate is illustrated in John 5 v 19 - 21:

Jesus gave them this answer: "I tell you the truth, the Son can do nothing by himself; he can do only what he sees his Father doing, because whatever the Father does the Son also does.

For the Father loves the Son and shows him all he does. Yes, to your amazement he will show him even greater things than these.

For just as the Father raises the dead and gives them life, even so the Son gives life to whom he is pleased to give it."

ONE WISH

Motive and purpose play a very important part in our decision making process.

Discovering our purpose is so crucial that it has made Rick Warren a best selling author with his book entitled *"The Purpose Driven Life"*.

Motive, on the other hand, is defined in the Chambers Dictionary as a consideration or emotion that excites to action.

What we say, what we desire, how we live, how we react, why we live, are all down to our purposes and motive. These actions can be driven by self-centeredness or God-centeredness, depending on the state of mind.

As Christians, it is very important to re-align our purpose and motive to be centred around God so that we not only please Him, but are fruitful.

King Solomon's purpose and motive meets this requirement as we can see in 1 King 3 v 9 -13:

"So give your servant a discerning heart to govern your people and to distinguish between right and wrong. For who is able to govern this great people of yours?"

The Lord was pleased that Solomon had asked for this. So God said to him, "Since you have asked for this and not for long life or wealth for yourself, nor have asked for the death of your enemies but for discernment in administering justice,

I will do what you have asked. I will give you a wise and discerning heart, so that there will never have been anyone like you, nor will there ever be.

Moreover, I will give you what you have not asked for - both riches and honour - so that in your lifetime you will have no equal among kings."

If you were granted a wish from God, would it be God-centred or self-centred?

MOTIVE AND PURPOSE PLAY A VERY IMPORTANT PART IN OUR DECISION MAKING PROCESS.

PANIC ROOM

We have all been faced with situations that have caused us to panic. During these times we are gripped with fear and most of the time we are not in control. The consequences of panicking can sometimes be a detrimental factor as highlighted by the definition of the word "panic".

"a sudden overwhelming fear, with or without cause, that produces hysterical or irrational behaviour, and that often spreads quickly through a group of persons or animals"

In Exodus 14 v 10 v 12, we see the panic stricken children of Israel as the chariots of Pharaoh approached them:

As Pharaoh approached, the Israelites looked up, and there were the Egyptians, marching after them. They were terrified and cried out to the LORD. They said to Moses, "Was it because there were no graves in Egypt that you brought us to the desert to die? What have you done to us by bringing us out of Egypt? Didn't we say to you in Egypt, 'Leave us alone; let us serve the Egyptians'? It would have been better for us to serve the Egyptians than to die in the desert!"

Their irrational behaviour preventing them from reacting based on the truth which was as Moses confirmed later that "the Egyptians whom ye have seen to day, ye shall see them again no more for ever! The Lord shall fight for you and ye shall hold your peace."

In situations that have the potential to cause us to panic, May the knowledge of God's promises grant us the peace that keeps us calm.

PHYSICIAN HEAL THYSELF

1. Is it feasible to assess your own character and say that you really know yourself in terms of what you can or cannot do?
2. Is it feasible to determine your reaction when you are faced with an unfamiliar situation?
3. Is it possible for you to assess yourself whether you are a good or bad person?

Amazing that we sometimes look aghast and surprised as we hear several stories of incidents that have involved our families, friends and third parties. We find ourselves making statements that involve the following phrases:

– "If it was me I would......"
– "How could they"

and other judgmental phrases we choose to compile. 1 Corinthians 4 v 3 – 5 gives us a stern warning about making judgments our potential reactions and leaving the final assessment to God, who knows in advance the state of your heart and your potential response:

I care very little if I am judged by you or by any human court; indeed, I do not even judge myself. My conscience

is clear, but that does not make me innocent. It is the Lord who judges me. Therefore judge nothing before the appointed time; wait till the Lord comes. He will bring to light what is hidden in darkness and will expose the motives of men's hearts. At that time each will receive his praise from God.

May the grace and mercy of God keep us in good standing in the blessed name of Jesus – Amen

PRACTICE MAKES PERFECT

'The message was powerful'; 'awesome message'; 'you have to get the tape' are clichés that we hear daily after the Word of God has been delivered.

The impact of a message cannot be determined until we apply it in our lives and see fruits or rewards as a result of that application. This can only occur by putting the Word of God into practice, as highlighted in Philippians 4 v 8 – 9:

Finally, brothers, whatever is true, whatever is noble, whatever is right, whatever is pure, whatever is lovely, whatever is admirable - if anything is excellent or praiseworthy - think about such things.

Whatever you have learned or received or heard from me, or seen in me - put it into practice. And the God of peace will be with you.

Application is what brings the benefits into our lives, as confirmed by scripture when God told the children of Israel that they had tarried at the mountain long enough.

REMEMBER THE TIMES

There is a saying that goes, 'Old things have passed away'.

In reality, the memories linger depending on the situation, and we need the divine grace of God to erase them from our memory banks.

Our memories should serve as an indicator of our former state, and in guiding new Christians or those still struggling with sin, we should always bear in mind that it was the grace that saw us through. Even though we may need to be firm, we have to do it with love and compassion. The importance of this approach is highlighted in Titus 3 v 3 – 5:

At one time we too were foolish, disobedient, deceived and enslaved by all kinds of passions and pleasures. We lived in malice and envy, being hated and hating one another. But when the kindness and love of God our Saviour appeared, He saved us, not because of righteous things we had done, but because of His mercy.

Remember the LORD's grace abounds to us all.

RESPONSE CENTRE

How do you respond to situations around you? Which of the following do you do?

a) Stop, Think and React
b) React, Think and Stop
c) Think, React and Stop

It seems the world around us is in such a hurry that we do not even have the patience to observe situations and ask the right questions. We are quick to presume we know the answers and then react accordingly; we presume to be good judges of character and categorise people according to our initial perceptions.

Most of my close friends are people that I saw in a different light at first, before I took the time to truly know who they were and what they were about.

In Acts 2 v 12 - 13 we see two responses to a situation that involved Jesus' disciples:

Amazed and perplexed, they asked one another, "What does this mean?"

Some, however, made fun of them and said, "They have had too much wine."

Looking at the response of the second set of people, you wonder whether they were the ones that served the wine, or whether they smelt the 'aroma' of wine on Peter's breath!

The first bit of advice I was given as a management consultant was to "Never assume – always ask questions if you do not understand." How many times do we second-guess God and prescribe how He will do something without consulting Him first?

I pray that God gives you the patience to stop, think and react!

SHINING EXAMPLE

There is a saying that goes 'First Impressions go a long way'.

As Christians either at home or in the marketplace, we shall always be under the microscope. The most effective way to bring people to Christ is through our character. What we do and say are important lamp posts that will lead people to Christ.

In Philippians 2 verses 14 – 16, we are advised on how to be effective lamp posts that shine to the glory of God:

Do everything without complaining or arguing, so that you may become blameless and pure, children of God without fault in a crooked and depraved generation, in which you shine like stars in the universe as you hold out the word of life - in order that I may boast on the day of Christ that I did not run or labour for nothing.

One of the ways effective communication is carried out is through observation. As we communicate to the world, let our actions speak louder than our words.

SOLUTION PROVIDER

After one of those days where you complain about every-thing and pray that the sun, moon and stars will quickly come down so you can move into the next day – I settled down to pray.

The Holy Spirit who has never let me down advised me of the following prayer:

"Train my lips to speak solutions and not problems"

As we know complaining does not achieve results unless you have a proposed solution. I remember advice given to me by a partner of the consulting firm I worked with "Always have a proposed solution to discuss when you bring the problem".

The beauty of this suggestion which we sometimes fail to realise is that the solution does not have to come from you, hence the whole notion of the concept called *"Research"*

We are also advised in Proverbs 8 v 6 – 10 on the role of our lips in providing godly solutions and not "problems"!

TRAIN MY LIPS TO SPEAK SOLUTIONS AND NOT PROBLEMS

Listen, for I will speak of excellent things, And from the opening of my lips will come right things; For my mouth will speak truth; Wickedness is an abomination to my lips. All the words of my mouth are with righteousness; Nothing crooked or perverse is in them. They are all plain to him who understands, And right to those who find knowledge. Receive my instruction, and not silver, And knowledge rather than choice gold.

SPECS SAVERS

The LORD has been speaking to me a lot about perception, and how you see things to gain a greater advantage.

In a book titled 'How to make it in business without losing your life' by Rob Parsons, he talks about Wayne Gresky, the greatest ice hockey player of all time. A sports psychologist pointed out that he differs from other great players because he has 40 degrees peripheral vision compared to other players, who have 20-25 degrees. In other words, he sees things other players do not see on the ice rink, which enables him negotiate outstanding moves and plays during matches.

What do you see and how do you see and perceive things in life? The importance of having clear vision and perspective is seen in the beginning, in Genesis 1 v 2 – 5:

Now the earth was formless and empty, darkness was over the surface of the deep, and the Spirit of God was hovering over the waters.

And God said, "Let there be light," and there was light.

God saw that the light was good and He separated the light from the darkness.

God called the light "day," and the darkness he called "night." And there was evening, and there was morning - the first day.

Light was needed to be able to grasp perspective and vision of the chaos that was on the earth at that stage.

Looking at things from a different angle - like Wayne Gresky - will enable you excel in all aspects of life because of your wider outlook on issues. It will also give you greater scope to make important decisions.

STEP BY STEP

The phrase 'A journey of a thousand miles begins with a single step' is often quoted.

The world has changed quite a lot over the last decade. There seem to be more tasks to carry out, which has led to the proliferation of Personal Digital Assistants (or PDAs) as we try to cram many tasks into a single day. The time management industry makes millions as they advise us on how to organise our lives to achieve maximum benefit.

In my opinion, the issue lies around the concept of short

term as opposed to long term. We now live in a 'microwave' society that wants everything to have been done yesterday!

Focusing on what really matters and taking the right steps to achieve it will eliminate a lot of clutter from our lives, and enable us complete the God-ordained tasks that have been assigned to us before the foundations of time.

How do we know the right steps to take?

One answer lies in Jeremiah 10 v 23 - 24:

I know, O Lord, that a man's life is not his own; it is not for man to direct his steps.

Correct me, Lord, but only with justice – not in your anger, less you reduce me to nothing.

Let us ask God to direct our steps and He will do so through the Holy Spirit, who has been appointed to be our Advisor and Counsellor and He will provide a step by step solution.

THE 80/20 RULE

I woke up today in one of those moods where you wish everything was in a certain way.

- I wish my wife was this or that;
- I wish the children were this or that;
- I wish my boss was this or that;
- I wish the church would do this or that;
- I wish I could afford this or that;

- I wish I could eat now;
- I wish the house was big, small, large, tidy etc. etc

So much wishful thinking that it took watching an edition of the Potters House to snap me out of this pity party - truly a word at the right time.

In this edition the speaker pointed out that in most cases – if we are true to ourselves - you will only achieve 80% satisfaction of what you really desire. The only one that can give you 100% is God and so we should seek Him for everything.

He gave an example of wives always complaining about the 20% of what their husbands are not and forget to appreciate the remaining 80%. He further went on to point out that we should appreciate the 80% of all what we have and stop spending our energies trying to achieve the 20% to the detriment of losing the whole 100%. Some men leave their wives in search of the 20% and when they achieve the 20% elsewhere, they suddenly realize that they have the 20% but have lost the 80% they had earlier.

A bit confusing – all these numbers but in reality that is the case. We should learn to appreciate what we have and God in his infinite wisdom will provide the rest.

THE "A" LIST

The dream of every aspiring actor and actress in Hollywood is to be named on the "A" List. A name on this list regardless of what number you are guarantees you a 6 figure income and access to the "influential" parties that will make or break your career. Staying on this list involves talking to the right people; attending the right award ceremonies; attending the right parties; acting in the right movies; and finally not offending the Hollywood movie moguls.

I do not know whether I would want to be on this list with so many "dos" and "don'ts". There is a list though that I would definitely want to be on which guarantees me everlasting life as highlighted in Revelation 22 v 14 - 15:

"Blessed are those who wash their robes, that they may have the right to the tree of life and may go through the gates into the city. Outside are the dogs, those who practice magic arts, the sexually immoral, the murderers, the idolaters and everyone who loves and practices falsehood.

So the choice is up to us as to which list we would prefer, the "list of death" or the "list of life". I pray that God enables us to make the right decision.

THE CHOSEN ONE

In a previous story we addressed the danger of incorrectly assessing a person's character before we ask for and get divine insight from God.

During one of our conferences a speaker pointed out that rather than criticize Osama bin Laden we should pray that he accepts Christ, as the impact on his followers would be massive. If he gave his life to God, the number of souls that would potentially be saved cannot be underestimated.

The example that comes to mind can be seen in Acts 9 verses 13 - 16, where God highlights His methodology for appointing people to carry out his assignments, and confirms yet again that His ways are not ours in the assessment of man's character:

"Lord," Ananias answered, "I have heard many reports about this man and all the harm he has done to your saints in Jerusalem.

And he has come here with authority from the chief priests to arrest all who call on your name."

But the Lord said to Ananias, "Go! This man is my chosen instrument to carry my name before the Gentiles and their kings and before the people of Israel.

I will show him how much he must suffer for my name."

Ananias was relying on man's report for his assessment, rather than the LORD's.

Whose report do you believe?

THE GREAT ESCAPE

The dictionary defines temptation as the *The desire to have or do something that you know you should avoid; "he felt the temptation and his will power weakened"*.

One of the greatest mistakes we often make is believing that temptations are a thing of the past once we're saved. Wrong! – You can be assured you that before the clock strikes two, you will be tempted to sin either in words, thoughts or deeds. Just when you think you have conquered a particular area – it comes back again. Ask Moses – his temptation in the area of anger came back to haunt him 40 years after the first encounter.

Look at all the great leaders who have fallen as this "master weapon" was wielded against them by the arch enemy. The greatest leader the world has ever seen was tempted in three major areas but he had a ready-made battle plan to conquer it. The enemy does not care where he uses this "weapon of mass destruction" – he will even use it on the church premises!

I remember a speaker who pointed out that he was on his way to engage in an illicit affair and the Holy Spirit warned him about the consequences. He highlighted the fact that the temptation was so strong he told the Holy Spirit that he couldn't follow him right then as he had some unfinished business.

Thank God for His mercy as his route to the "unfinished business" was blocked at every access point. 1 Corinthians 10 v 12 – 13 gives us an escape route when the enemy comes in like a flood:

Therefore let him who thinks he stands take heed lest he fall. No temptation has overtaken you except such as is common to man; but God is faithful, who will not allow

you to be tempted beyond what you are able, but with the temptation will also make the way of escape, that you may be able to bear it.

May the Holy Spirit open our eyes to see every escape route to temptation.

THE HUMILITY TEST

One of the most important characteristics a teacher must possess is humility.

There is the danger of contentment with the status quo, especially if you are a leader that possesses global influence and you command a great level of respect. You may begin to feel you are so knowledgeable on a subject there is no need to learn any more.

The book of James gives us a stern warning on the subject of teaching. He points out that not many of us should become teachers, knowing that we will receive a stricter judgment. The Humility Test addresses the following question:

With the great influence and respect you have achieved, are you humble enough to accept correction when you are wrong?

At first, we may all answer 'Yes', but consider that you have just preached the message of your life to thousands, only to discover from a third party that the accuracy of your message could be improved with a little more research into a part of the Bible that is not your forté?

We see an example in Acts 18 v24 – 26:

Meanwhile a Jew named Apollos, a native of Alexandria, came to Ephesus. He was a learned man, with a thorough knowledge of the Scriptures.

He had been instructed in the way of the Lord, and he spoke with great fervor and taught about Jesus accurately, though he knew only the baptism of John.

He began to speak boldly in the synagogue. When Priscilla and Aquila heard him, they invited him to their home and explained to him the way of God more adequately.

Later in the passage we see Apollo becoming a more seasoned preacher, teaching that Jesus is the Christ and helping all those that believed through grace.

We must never reach a stage in our lives where we feel we know enough, because growth determines who we are.

THE NEW IMPROVED VERSION

Companies understand the importance of continuous improvement in products they market to consumers.

Millions are spent on advertising to convey the message that the latest modifications to their products make them better in quality and functionality. This whole process of re-branding involves taking an improved product, re-naming it and marketing it as a new and improved version.

This is similar to the circumcision process we go through with the aid of the Holy Spirit. The power of the Holy Spirit works in us internally to improve our character, and re-brands us by renewing our minds and hearts, as highlighted in Romans 2 v 28 – 29:

A man is not a Jew if he is only one outwardly, nor is circumcision merely outward and physical.

No, a man is a Jew if he is one inwardly; and circumcision is circumcision of the heart, by the Spirit, not by the written code. Such a man's praise is not from men, but from God.

The re-branding makes us a new creation in Christ Jesus, as we begin to think, speak and act differently.

THE PEACEMAKER

Peace is defined in the Chambers dictionary as the following:

- Harmonious relations
- Freedom from disputes
- The absence of mental stress or anxiety.

Achieving this state of mind is absolutely essential if we are to be effective in our daily walk, as we are subjected to large amounts of decision-making throughout the day. Decisions that affect our marital status, careers, health, finances and other critical areas are made under all kinds of pressure from the world.

One of the best pieces of advice I have received was from a senior manager within the company. "Sleep over every major decision, and avoid making critical decisions under pressure". Easier said than done, but past experience shows that we have all made decisions for which we are still bearing the consequences.

How do we get that peace that ensures we have harmonious relationships, eradicate disputes and free our minds from stress or anxiety? The answer lies in what Jesus did before every decision He made. He sought the will of His Father, Who provides the peace we need on a daily basis, as seen in Philippians 4 v 6 - 7:

Do not be anxious about anything, but in everything, by prayer and petition, with thanksgiving, present your requests to God.

And the peace of God, which transcends all understanding, will guard your hearts and your minds in Christ Jesus.

"SLEEP OVER EVERY MAJOR DECISION, AND AVOID MAKING CRITICAL DECISIONS UNDER PRESSURE"

Sleep, in the context of the senior manager's advice, can mean presenting the issue to God, relaxing and waiting for His answer prior to implementation.

THE POWER OF REPENTANCE

News-Flash

It was an unbelievable sight at the Jesus House Centre in Baghdad as Osama Bin Laden and Sadaam Hussein in front of thousands of worshippers repented of their sins and gave their lives to Jesus Christ.

There was mixed reaction as two camps emerged as to whether God could truly forgive these men for their wicked acts. Some questioned whether it was true repentance or a publicity stunt.

I leave you to ponder on these thoughts but in 1 Kings 21 v 27 - 28, we see the reward of the true repentance of an individual who had performed wicked acts:

So it was, when Ahab heard those words, that he tore his clothes and put sackcloth on his body, and fasted and lay in sackcloth, and went about mourning. And the word of the LORD came to Elijah the Tishbite, saying, See how Ahab has humbled himself before Me? Because he has humbled himself before Me, I will not bring the calamity in his days. In the days of his son I will bring the calamity on his house."

What do you think now that you have read God's "school of thought"?

THE SCHOOL OF HARD KNOCKS

School attendance is a must!

The normal sequence of events is that you attend school in the following stages: Nursery, Primary, Secondary and University. Not everyone is privileged to go through and complete them all, but one school that you will attend regardless of your social status is The School of Life, or as some people call it, The School of Hard Knocks.

This school takes you through tutorials that you may not have covered in the course of your formal education. This school will either break you or make you. It will either mould or destroy your character, but what is certain is that everyone goes through it, and how you respond to its teachings is up to you!

The Bible gives us an insight into some lectures you will have to go through in Romans 5 v 3 – 5:

Not only so, but we also rejoice in our sufferings, because we know that suffering produces perseverance; perseverance, character; and character, hope.

And hope does not disappoint us, because God has poured out his love into our hearts by the Holy Spirit, whom he has given us.

The advantage that we have as Christians is that the Holy Spirit is our 'textbook' as He guides us along the way. May the Word of God be a lamp unto our feet and a light unto our path.

TO BOAST IS TO ROAST!

One of the most dangerous statements to make as a Christian is "I am self-made in every aspect of my life". Not acknowledging the hand of God in your life could be the wrong move because life will always throw you a "curve ball" which will require God being the master "batsman or hitter". The dangerous thing about boasting in oneself is the fact that it comes in a subtle form. How many times do we hear the following "credentials" on books and major events?

- Anointed man of God who attracts signs and wonders;
- Powerful man of God;
- Author of over 50 best selling books
- Oversees a church of over 30,000 members.

Alternatively when you watch some of the "promotions" to the events you hear statements like the following:

- 'When Pastor X prayed for me.......'
- Send $50 and you will receive a "blessed handkerchief" which Pastor X has prayed over – expect your blessings and miracle

Question: Is the information above "optional" or "mandatory"?

In my humble opinion, these statements can border on the lines of boasting in self rather than in the Lord. As a servant of God pointed out at a recent meeting – once you start believing in these accolades, that is the first step on the path to destruction.

We should take a leaf from Apostle Paul who understood the dangers and chose to acknowledge God in all his ways as highlighted in 2 Corinthians v 7 – 10:

To keep me from becoming conceited because of these surpassingly great revelations, there was given me a thorn in my flesh, a messenger of Satan, to torment me. Three times I pleaded with the Lord to take it away from me. But he said to me, "My grace is sufficient for you, for my power is made perfect in weakness." Therefore I will boast all the more gladly about my weaknesses, so that Christ's power may rest on me. That is why, for Christ's sake, I delight in weaknesses, in insults, in hardships, in persecutions, in difficulties. For when I am weak, then I am strong.

Even when he introduced himself to the various congregations – he acknowledged his total reliance on God in his opening speech as highlighted in the examples below:

- **"Paul, a bondservant of Jesus Christ"**
- **"Paul, called to be an apostle of Jesus Christ through the will of God"**
- **"Paul, an apostle (not from men not through man, but through Jesus Christ and God the Father"**

Let us learn to boast in the Lord to prevent unnecessary roasting that comes from the thorn. Thank God that his grace is sufficient!

TREMORS

An interesting thought came to my mind a couple of weeks ago about the number of Christians who claim to be born again.

While I was thinking about this, a question popped into my mind.

Do those of us that claim to be born again really know God?

I think the answer to the question is crucial, because believing in God is not enough as confirmed in James 2 v 19:

"You believe that there is one God. Good! Even the demons believe that – and shudder"

How do our actions confirm our belief in God? Do we truly fear and reverence God in spirit and in truth, or do we believe in Him like the demons do, but then just shudder and disobey Him?

We would gain immensely from emulating Abraham who believed and obeyed God, so that it can be credited to us as righteousness.

TRIAL RUN

While praying at a meeting, I felt compassion for couples believing God for a child.

I asked Him why they had to go through the whole process of waiting. The response I got was very insightful. I was pointed to Hebrews, which is often called the 'Hall of Faith' because it lists men and women of faith who triumphed in their lifetime.

By faith these people offered sacrifices, obeyed and left one place for another, were taken away so they would not see death, passed through the Red Sea, marched around the walls of Jericho and so on. Hebrews 11 v 39 – 40 sums it all by encouraging us with the following statement:

And all these, having obtained a good testimony through faith, did not receive the promise, God having provided something better for us, that they should not be made perfect apart from us.

He further went on to say that without these people there would be no 'Hall of Faith'. He takes people through all sorts of trials from marriage, financial, emotional, health and more so there will always be entries in the 'Hall of Faith' which can serve as a reference point of encouragement for our era.

Everyone's trial is unique; what He takes you through may be different from what He takes someone else through.

The assurance He gives us is that His grace shall be sufficient for each of us during the process!

UNIQUE SELLING POINT

While surfing channels on telly to find something to watch, my fingers stopped when I got to a program called Celebrity Love Island.

After watching about five minutes of it, I began to ponder on what is currently allowed on television compared to what had been allowed in times past.

During the era of the late Mary Whitehouse – a famous activist against immorality on television – she would have kicked up a fuss over such a program, which is based on unmarried couples taking turns on dates to determine their compatibility.

The Word of God confirms that this concept is not acceptable, and it is just another example of how the enemy has subtly wielded his influence through the most effective form of communication over the years – the media.

I am not advocating mass demonstrations, but we should be aware and make a stand in our own little way. It can start from our places of work: by watching what we say, how we react and the issues we support. It took twelve people to influence the world through the impact of their characters, words and deeds – so can we!

What is that unique selling point that makes us stand out in the world? What do they see in our attitude that attracts and amazes them?

Examples of selling points are highlighted in Ephesians 4 v 20 – 24:

You, however, did not come to know Christ that way.

Surely you heard of him and were taught in him in accordance with the truth that is in Jesus.

You were taught, with regard to your former way of life, to put off your old self, which is being corrupted by its deceitful desires;

to be made new in the attitude of your minds; and to put on the new self, created to be like God in true righteousness and holiness.

When our friends or those around us see positive changes, it will make them ponder their ways and by God's grace, get them to renew their minds and change their attitudes to accept Christ in their lives.

This will filter to the marketplace, and eventually, to all areas where the Gospel will make a major impact. May God give us the grace and wisdom to take a stand!

WALKING TALL

Here we go again, you are upset and agent 'flesh' loves every minute of it. He knows that this is the opportunity to inflict total damage to your walk in Christ. The silent voice of the Holy Spirit calmly tells you to pray but because you are so mad, you ignore and allow the aggressive voice of the flesh to commence 'collateral damage'.

In advance of your arrival to work, the enemy has sent his own version of the Special Air Service (SAS) to plant 'fleshly mines' in the form of anger, seductive secretary, and an obnoxious colleague to inflict more damage. As you get in the car, the calm voice advises you to shore up your defence by praying with him. Again this advice is ignored as you drive yourself to the impending danger in the form of the "welcome committee" of the enemy.

You arrive at work to find the seductive secretary so attractive that you can't think straight as you make numerous errors while trying to balance the company accounts. To make matters worse the boss hears some conflicting information about your performance and issues you with an ultimatum to get your act together. Now because secret agent "anger" has been placed in the office – you lash out at your boss and storm out of the office to go home.

It doesn't get better as you arrive home and the enemy has done advanced research to manipulate those closest to you as to which buttons to press to take you over the edge. At this stage, you can't hear the calm voice anymore and begin to contemplate on whether there is a God.

YOU IGNORE AND ALLOW THE AGGRESSIVE VOICE OF THE FLESH TO COMMENCE 'COLLATERAL DAMAGE'.

The answer is that there is a God who has sent his Holy Spirit as that calm voice and he has advised us in Galatians 5 v 16 – 18 and v 22 – 25 on the most effective strategy to combat the enemy during our daily walk!

So I say, live by the Spirit, and you will not gratify the desires of the sinful nature. For the sinful nature desires what is contrary to the Spirit, and the Spirit what is contrary to the sinful nature. They are in conflict with each other, so that you do not do what you want. But if you are led by the Spirit, you are not under law.

But the fruit of the Spirit is love, joy, peace, patience, kindness, goodness, faithfulness, gentleness and self-control. Against such things there is no law. Those who belong to Christ Jesus have crucified the sinful nature with its passions and desires. Since we live by the Spirit, let us keep in step with the Spirit.

WHAT DO YOU DESIRE?

The blame culture started in the Garden of Eden, when Mr. Adam refused to accept responsibility for creating an environment which facilitated the disobedience of Mrs. Eve. The third party involved in the events which transpired was the crafty creature called Mr. Satan, also known as 'The Devil'. He has been bombarding us with his subtle strategies since that infamous day.

An American hit show in the 70's called *The Flip Wilson Show* had a character called Geraldine who was always saying "the devil made me do it". Man's refusal to take responsibility is a topic that can be discussed until the LORD comes.

If we are going to survive the onslaught of the enemy, we have to recognise and accept our faults, and commit them to the Lord.

You cannot be tempted by something you do not like. The areas we are most likely to be tempted are in the areas of our addictions, or to put in slightly milder terms, our desires. This is highlighted in James 1 v 13 - 15:

When tempted, no one should say, "God is tempting me." For God cannot be tempted by evil, nor does he tempt anyone; but each one is tempted when, by his own evil desire, he is dragged away and enticed. Then, after desire has conceived, it gives birth to sin; and sin, when it is fully grown, gives birth to death.

WHERE EAGLES DARE!

One cannot underestimate the revenue the pharmaceutical industry generates from meeting the needs of people trying to combat tiredness.

In an attempt to maximise the twenty-four hours God's grace guarantees us each day, people work flat out, sustaining themselves on these products. Coffee manufacturing firms are also big players, as the caffeine can provide a short-term solution that keeps us from visiting 'dreamland'.

How do we combat 'spiritual tiredness'?

The good news is that God's solution in Isaiah 40 v 28 – 31 provides both a physical and spiritual remedy:

Do you not know? Have you not heard? The LORD is the everlasting God, the Creator of the ends of the earth. He will not grow tired or weary, and his understanding no one can fathom.

He gives strength to the weary and increases the power of the weak.

Even youths grow tired and weary, and young men stumble and fall; but those who hope in the LORD will renew their strength. They will soar on wings like eagles; they will run and not grow weary, they will walk and not be faint.

Tiredness indicates that we need to take a well deserved break to recharge those tired cells. We should not seek to resist the process, as it will always come to pass.

Perhaps I could sell this solution to the pharmaceutical industry to reduce their development costs!

WHERE HAS ALL THE TIME GONE?

We are at the beginning of March, and we are probably wondering why the year seems to be going so fast.

If we were asked to recollect what we have accomplished this year, most of us will struggle. As I wrote this, I asked myself - where has all the time gone and why can't I account for it? I should be able to account for at least fifty percent of that time.

While my brain was trying to get an accurate day by day account like a computer memory chip, the Holy Spirit pointed me to the following Scripture in Luke 4 v 18 - 20:

"The Spirit of the Lord is upon me, because he has anointed me to preach the gospel to the poor; he hath sent me to heal the broken hearted, to preach deliverance to the captives, and recovering of sight to the blind, to set at liberty them that are bruised.

To preach the acceptable year of the Lord."

And He closed the book.

The reason why an accurate account could be given of Jesus' activities was that they were in line with His overall mission on earth. Every task could be assigned to the categories highlighted in His mission statement, as can be seen in the above Scripture.

We need to adopt the same policy by drafting a mission statement that encompasses all our activities, so that at any point in the year we can give an accurate account of our lives.

WHITE LIE

In my quest for knowledge I looked up the definition for a "white lie" in the dictionary and the results are detailed below:

1. a minor, polite, or harmless lie; fib;
2. An often trivial, diplomatic or well-intentioned untruth;
3. An untruth told to spare feelings or from politeness, as in She asked if I liked her dress, and of course I told a white lie. This term uses white in the sense of "harmless;
4. an unimportant lie (especially one told to be tactful or polite).

The word of interest in the various definitions is "harmless". When did a lie become harmless? Interestingly enough – the same dictionary defines a "lie" as the following:

1. a false statement made with deliberate intent to deceive; an intentional untruth; a falsehood;
2. an inaccurate or false statement;
3. to speak falsely or utter untruth knowingly, as with intent to deceive;
4. something intended or serving to convey a false impression.

From the definition above, a lie is far from being "harmless". If we make reference to our "spiritual dictionary" – we see that the consequences of lying is far from "harmless" as highlighted in Revelation 21 v 8:

But the cowardly, the unbelieving, the vile, the murderers, the sexually immoral, those who practice magic arts, the idolaters and all liars—their place will be in the fiery lake of burning sulfur. This is the second death."

WORD PROCESSOR

Scenario - 1. Back in the days, examinations were interesting times. I always used to wonder what people were writing as the phrase "more paper" used to echo in the air. It was even more frightening during tough papers like for example - "Pure Mathematics" that you questioned whether you and the person attended the same lectures.

Scenario - 2. It has been highlighted that the ratio of words that a woman speaks to that spoken by her male counterpart is in the region of three to one. Some may even argue the case that as a result their vocabulary is better than men.

Scenario - 3. How many words per minute is a question most secretaries are familiar with as they prepare their CV's for potential job offers. One of the most critical success factors for theses type of jobs is the speed in which documents can be produced hence this important ratio.

It's all about "the number of words" the three scenarios above seem to imply but Proverbs 30 v 5 - 6 gives us a further insight into the importance of quality and not quantity when it comes to words.

Every word of God is flawless; He is a shield to those who take refuge in Him. Do not add to His words, or He will rebuke you and prove you a liar.

WYSIWYG

If you are thinking that the title above is in a foreign language, you are wrong!

It is an acronym for 'what you see is what you get.' This is a computer application that enables you to see on screen exactly what will appear when the document is printed.

When people see us, do they see the character of Jesus in us or are we just replicas of the Dr Jekyll and Mr. Hyde character – split personalities? Do people want to spew us out because we are neither hot nor cold? Progression requires stability, and this comes from consistency. An example of this acronym can be seen in Jesus' life as highlighted in Colossians 1 v 15 – 16 and John 5 v 19 – 20:

He is the image of the invisible God, the firstborn over all creation.

For by Him all things were created: things in heaven and on earth, visible and invisible, whether thrones or powers or rulers or authorities; all things were created by Him and for Him.

Jesus gave them this answer: "I tell you the truth, the Son can do nothing by Himself; He can do only what he sees his Father doing, because whatever the Father does the Son also does.

For the Father loves the Son and shows Him all He does. Yes, to your amazement He will show Him even greater things than these.

What we see in God is exactly what we get from our LORD Jesus.

YEAR END APPRAISAL

We are fast approaching year end and most companies will be taking stock of not just their inventories but a general assessment of their performance. The results serve as a benchmark for them to make adjustments to their long term or medium term strategic plans.

At this point in time, most employees would have had their appraisals carried out and depending on the result – "Christmas Expenditure" could be heavy or light as the employer decides whether you have done enough to be rewarded.

On the other hand you may have to be content with the phrase "Come Back Next Year".

As a Christian, there is one phrase that we so desire from our Heavenly Father as coined in Matthew 3 v 16 - 17:

As soon as Jesus was baptized, He went up out of the water. At that moment heaven was opened, and He saw the Spirit of God descending like a dove and lighting on Him. And a voice from heaven said, "This is my Son, whom I love; with Him I am well pleased."

This year end, let us review our walk with Christ and prepare for the coming year so that every day we are happy knowing that God is pleased with the way we walk and the way we talk.

PART 3

RELATIONSHIP WITH PEOPLE

7 NEWS

More Breaking News!

- Earthquake in South East Asia claiming thousand of lives;
- AIDS epidemic sees no near end solution;
- US launches counter-attack against Iraq to defend the Saudi Arabia kingdom;
- Famine in Africa reaches an alarming level;
- United Nations in futile attempt to prevent the development of nuclear weapons by Iran to ensure peace in the Middle East.

When I hear such news, I ask myself, should I abandon watching the bulletin and focus only on the good news offered by the Bible ? The answer is No. We cannot isolate ourselves from what is going on around us. The news gives us issues on which to focus our prayers on.

Thank God for the blessed assurance we have in Luke 21 v 36 on how to respond to the events around us as predicted in Luke 21 v 10 – 11:

Then he said to them: "Nation will rise against nation, and kingdom against kingdom. There will be great earthquakes, famines and pestilences in various places, and fearful events and great signs from heaven.

The words of encouragement highlighted in Luke 21 v 36 are the following:

Be always on the watch, and pray that you may be able to escape all that is about to happen, and that you may be able to stand before the Son of Man."

We all remember the motto of the Boys Scouts – Be prepared!

AMAZING GRACE

The word 'amazing' according to the Dictionary is defined as the following:

- to overwhelm with surprise or sudden wonder; astonish greatly;
- To cause great wonder or astonishment: a sight that amazes.

This was my reaction on my first project when a Senior Consultant was flown in from England to save a project that was near doom. Upon his arrival the skill and expertise that was exhibited was so wonderfully crafted that only the comforting words of my manager "that he has been doing this for a long time" – kept me at peace.

There is something about demonstrating the influence of wisdom, excellence and skill that keeps people asking questions as highlighted in Matthew 13 v 53 – 54:

When Jesus had finished these parables (these comparisons), He left there. And coming to His own country [Nazareth], He taught in their synagogue so that

they were amazed with bewildered wonder, and said, Where did this Man get this wisdom and these miraculous powers? Is not this the carpenter's Son? Is not His mother called Mary? And are not His brothers James and Joseph and Simon and Judas? And do not all His sisters live here among us? Where then did this Man get all this?

These are the competitive advantages that give us that extra edge as we journey along the path of success. It will bring us before kings and not mediocre and mere men.

ASSOCIATION OF TEACHERS

Flyers, billboards, internet adverts, workshops, and lectures all highlight the fact that everyone has something to share or express.

In other words, we can all claim to be teachers. This may be the case, but the Bible gives a stern warning to those that profess to be teachers.

There is more to assuming the role that must be taken into consideration, like the answer to this question:

How effective is your teaching or message?

Nowadays, everyone wants to move from being an 'apprentice' to 'expert' status overnight.

When Jesus delivered His sermons, the crowds were always amazed that He taught as one who had authority. On the other hand, when the religious scholars taught they always cited traditions and quoted authorities to support their arguments and convince the people.

To be an effective teacher, one should imitate the style of Jesus by adopting authority and originality, rather than manipulation as confirmed in Matthew 7 v 28 - 29:

"When Jesus had finished saying these things, the crowds were amazed at his teaching, because he taught as one who had authority, and not as their teachers of the law.

BABY TALK

There is a school of thought which implies that children should be seen and not heard. In other words "Keep Quiet". Below is an extract from Jonathan Aitken's book called *Pride and Perjury* which highlights a different point of view.

"Yet even in this ceaseless round of activity, William could not fail to catch glimpses of my distress. One night, as we were consuming our hamburgers and Budweiser beers under a spectacularly clear Milky Way in the heavens above us, I asked him obliquely whether he thought his own life and future career might have rather better prospects if he was not encumbered with the burden of a disgraced father hovering in the background. "Don't be a chump, Daddy," he replied.

"Even the Guardian can't keep you in the doghouse for ever. You'll find plenty to do. Besides, I need you."

This single statement from his son contributed to him not committing suicide and pressing forward to find out God's will for his life.

God can use your children to impart timely knowledge, understanding and wisdom into your life when you least expect it as highlighted in Psalm 8 v 2:

Out of the mouth of babes and nursing infants You have ordained strength,   Because of Your enemies, That You may silence the enemy and the avenger.

CASE LAW

Death is not a topic that we all like to talk about but it will happen at God's appointed time. It will be the day that we are all judged on how we have treated God's people and an appraisal of our assignment on earth.

We are advised that every idle word spoken will be taken into account. Every time we have made false accusations and judgments – the role will be reversed as the Almighty God will become the Judge and Jury.

This is highlighted in Romans 14 v 10-14

But why do you judge your brother? Or why do you show contempt for your brother? For we shall all stand before the judgment seat of Christ. For it is written As I live, says the LORD, Every knee shall bow to Me, And every tongue shall confess to God. So then each of us shall give account of himself to God. Therefore let us not judge one another anymore, but rather resolve this, not to put a stumbling block or a cause to fall in our brother's way.

DEATH IS NOT A TOPIC THAT WE ALL LIKE TO TALK ABOUT BUT IT WILL HAPPEN AT GOD'S APPOINTED TIME.

Let us learn to be encouragers and motivators in Christ through our conversation so that every word we speak can be reconciled to the Word of God.

CHIEF PROTOCOL OFFICER

I was involved in a discussion about the level of security imposed by the so-called protocol officers in church, who can sometimes be more intimidating than the Secret Service.

Surely - one participant exclaimed - "God can look after his own". Another echoed, "What are the angels for?"

I would be careful about passing judgment on pastors who opt for this approach. Not a lot of time should be spent discussing this, as there are weightier matters in the church that deserve attention, such as the salvation of souls and the propagation of the gospel to a global market.

On the flip side though, there can be occasions when these protocol officers can hinder the operations of God. "Book an appointment", "The reception is only for pastors", "Are you a pastor?" are typical responses by the officers as they seek to restrict access to the man of God.

We have to remember that in the eyes of God we are one, and God can use anyone regardless of their title in His wide sphere of operations – which may include getting a message to the man of God.

One of the dangers of not discerning the potential move of God and causing restrictions is highlighted in Numbers 11 v 26 – 30:

However, two men, whose names were Eldad and Medad, had remained in the camp. They were listed among the elders, but did not go out to the Tent. Yet the Spirit also rested on them, and they prophesied in the camp. A young man ran and told Moses, "Eldad and Medad are prophesying in the camp.

Joshua son of Nun, who had been Moses' aide since youth, spoke up and said, "Moses, my lord, stop them!"

But Moses replied, "Are you jealous for my sake? I wish that all the LORD's people were prophets and that the LORD would put his Spirit on them!" Then Moses and the elders of Israel returned to the camp.

We need to discern when God is moving and how He moves, so we do not pose a hindrance. Remember, God used a donkey!

CHILD OF INNOCENCE

One cannot underestimate the level of damage that the break down between parents and their children has caused in the present day society. We ask ourselves 'what has happened to respect for elders or child innocence? Children as young as thirteen giving birth. In the US, children can "divorce" their parents. Teenage gangs pose more threat than the Al Qaeda!

This is also not helped by the "immunity" children get from the government – some which are helpful, others which are detrimental. I ask myself, if a child has killed an adult and you claim that the name of the child has to be with-held to protect the child - then who protects the adult?

As I pondered about these scenarios – I asked myself the question:

What has caused this breakdown?

I belive that one of the factors is that parents do not take the time to understand their children. Most of us were brought up in the era where a child was "only seen" and "not heard". This can result in a lot of frustration in a child as all forms of expressional outlets are blocked.

The Bible in Luke 2 v 48 – 50 and Luke 8 v 20 – 21 highlights the importance of listening to our children and pondering over what they have said before we react. It stresses the need for us to try and understand our children and where they are coming from:

When his parents saw him, they were astonished. His mother said to him, "Son, why have you treated us like this? Your father and I have been anxiously searching for you." "Why were you searching for me?" he asked.

"Didn't you know I had to be in my Father's house?" But they did not understand what he was saying to them. Then he went down to Nazareth with them and was obedient to them. But his mother treasured all these things in her heart.

Someone told him, "Your mother and brothers are standing outside, wanting to see you." He replied, "My mother and brothers are those who hear God's word and put it into practice."

Be Honest – what will your first reaction be if your child responded to your questions in this manner? Will you ponder for a greater understanding or will you blunder for a lack of understanding?

CHILD PROTECTION ACT

Not again! Not another case where a child has gone missing.

How could they! Another case where a gang of youths have attacked an elderly person.

Can you imagine? A child divorces his parents in a US court!

Our children are our future so naturally we care about them, but there is only so much we can do to protect them from a degenerating society. Sometimes, our overprotection can lead to rebellion as we restrict children's freedom.

I clearly remember how many times I sneaked out of school and out of the house without my parent's knowledge or approval! A child even going to church regularly with their parents does not guarantee safety from negative exposure, as MTV and other influences still find a way into their repertoire of viewing material.

How can we protect our children without going overboard?

An excellent answer is found in Proverbs 14 v 26:

He who fears the LORD has a secure fortress, and for his children it will be a refuge.

CHURCH-LIFE BALANCE

In the corporate world, after a series of fatal heart attacks, divorces, frustration, lack of bonding between husbands and wives, parents and children, and finally with the intervention of the European Union Court based in Brussels, organisations are beginning to recognise that we all need to have a life outside the workplace.

Employees are being encouraged to have the right balance between home life and work in order to maintain harmony and improve their efficiency.

My organisation does a lot in this area, especially as my job sometimes entails being away from home for long periods. Work-life balance is addressed by the firm in its policy of making arrangements for my family to travel to visit me periodically.

In my opinion, this issue does not just affect the workplace. It can and does happen in the church. Numerous conferences and meetings take their toll on individuals, and we need to be secure in ourselves to recognise that we do not need to attend every event.

EMPLOYEES ARE BEING ENCOURAGED
TO HAVE THE RIGHT BALANCE BETWEEN
HOME LIFE AND WORK IN ORDER
TO MAINTAIN HARMONY AND
IMPROVE THEIR EFFICIENCY.

Church, as described in certain sections of the Bible is the gathering of people, which can happen anywhere. In other words, it can be held in the pub, on a football pitch, a cafe or at any location where there are two or more, as long as the Word of God is being shared.

Before we burn ourselves out, we need to seek God's wisdom, knowledge, and understanding, and follow His strategy in Genesis 2 v 2 - 3:

By the seventh day God had finished the work he had been doing; so on the seventh day he rested from all his work.

And God blessed the seventh day and made it holy, because on it he rested from all the work of creating that he had done.

That's right: we need to build into our heavy schedules time to rest and address other areas of our lives, to ensure the balance is right and to keep us stable and effective.
LORD, help us to get a life!

CLASS STRUGGLE

While reading a glossy magazine on the luxurious Bentley car brand, I began to question whether I would really enjoy the lifestyle associated with the rich and so-called upper class.

Joining the hockey club, speaking in a certain way, the never-ending dinner invites, picking the right political parties, and finally, having a double-barrelled name.

It is amazing and frightening that society has assigned people to classes and expects them to stay in their place. So, we have the following 'classes' of people: rich and poor, lower class, middle class and upper class, 'happening' people and 'not so happening' people...I could go on and on but I won't!

In Colossians 3 v 9 - 11, we are encouraged to see the fallacy of basing our lives on what class we belong to, or on 'cliques':

Do not lie to each other, since you have taken off your old self with its practices

And have put on the new self, which is being renewed in knowledge in the image of its Creator.

Here there is no Greek or Jew, circumcised or uncircumcised, barbarian, Scythian, slave or free, but Christ is all, and is in all.

The message of Christ has eliminated and torn down all barriers created by man. We should all belong to the 'class' of Christ.

CONFLICT RESOLUTION

It was a normal day for Mr. and Mrs. Smith as they made their way to the counselor for yet another attempt at healing their marriage. As they arrived at the office, they saw a note stuck on the door with the inscription "READ PROVERBS 15 v 1-2 and get back to me with your thoughts".

They were confused as they had not read the Bible in a long time because of the constant bickering that went on in their house. They got home and they both agreed to have a shot at reading this scripture:

"A soft answer turns away wrath, but a harsh word stirs up anger. The tongue of the wise uses knowledge rightly, but the mouth of the fool pours forth foolishness.

Intrigued by the scripture they called the counselor and requested for further clarification. He advised them to buy a copy of the "The Maxwell Leadership Bible" and turn to page 761 for a detailed analysis of the scripture. In obedience they rushed to the Pages Bookshop to buy a copy and sat down to read and digest the explanation.

- Remain calm and gentle when confronting conflict, and your example will become contagious
- Speak wisely, making sure your information is truthful and accurate

- Remember, God is the ultimate Judge and will execute justice
- Use your words to foster healing; fix the problem, not the blame
- Stay teachable; be open to correction and quick to apologise when wrong
- Add value to everyone who contacts you, even when you disagree
- Speak words that spread knowledge and understanding

The advice really paid off as Mr. and Mrs. Smith are still together 50 years after that eventful day.

CUSTOMER SERVICE

The most important departments in any organizations are the ones that deal directly with people. Millions are spent yearly as firms ensure that the paying customer will continue to engage in "repeat" sales as a result of good service. The wrong word, thought or deed towards a customer can have massive implications for any organisation – ask Gerald Ratner if he would ever tell the customer that they are buying "crap".

The main reason I travel on British Airways is the pre-flight customer treatment at the airport lounge. It takes away a lot of my nerves and makes me feel relaxed before every flight.

As humans we like to be treated with respect and dignity which transcends to what we expect from any individual or organisation.

In Genesis 18 v 2 - 5, we see the Spirit needed to facilitate effective customer service

He looked up and noticed three men standing nearby. When he saw them, he ran to meet them and welcomed them, bowing low to the ground. "My lord," he said, "if it pleases you, stop here for a while. Rest in the shade of this tree while water is brought to wash your feet. And since you've honored your servant with this visit, let me prepare some food to refresh you before you continue on your journey." "All right," they said. "Do as you have said."

The extent to which Abraham went to ensure that he was the perfect host was cemented in v 8:

When the food was ready, Abraham took some yogurt and milk and the roasted meat, and he served it to the men.

As they ate, Abraham waited on them in the shade of the trees.

Remember the famous phrase "Do unto others as you want them to do for you"

ETIQUETTE 101

You have everything mapped out. Wake up early - skip breakfast to save time and have a heavy lunch at the wedding scheduled for 2pm. You marvel at the "time -

management" skills of the wedding planner as everything is going like clock work. You calculate that at this rate – you will be delving into a nice plate of rice, peas and any other assortments on the buffet table by 4.30 – Wrong!

At 4.30 you are told that the couple are still taking photographs and the schedule for serving of the food has been changed to accommodate the couple and their family. At this stage your stomach is on "hunger alert" and your flesh is on "anger alert".

I feel for you as I have been in this situation before but now I believe I am more the wiser after coming across 1 Corinthians 11 v 33 – 34:

So then, my brothers, when you come together to eat, wait for each other. If anyone is hungry, he should eat at home, so that when you meet together it may not result in judgment.

FAVOUR AIN'T FAIR

I am struggling with accepting some practices that go on in churches based on wealth and status. Consider the following scenarios:

1. Accepting offerings from people who have gained their wealth from questionable sources, and elevating their statuses in the church by placing them in positions of authority.

2. Reserving front row seats for people of so-called 'high status'.
3. Extending this 'service' to their children and other people associated with them.
4. High ranking officials in the church demanding privileges because of their positions.
5 Leaders flouting regulations that are in place to facilitate order and structure.

I often wonder, what happened to the concept of servant-leadership? We are warned in James 2 v 1 – 4 about the issue of favouritism:

My brothers, as believers in our glorious Lord Jesus Christ, don't show favouritism.

Suppose a man comes into your meeting wearing a gold ring and fine clothes, and a poor man in shabby clothes also comes in.

If you show special attention to the man wearing fine clothes and say, "Here's a good seat for you," but say to the poor man, "You stand there" or "Sit on the floor by my feet,"

Have you not discriminated among yourselves and become judges with evil thoughts?

This can happen at all levels within the church and we need to be careful because in the eyes of the LORD we are all one, and relationships form one of the most important bedrocks of Christianity.

HAPPY PEOPLE

The importance of relationships and people could not be emphasized more than it was in a quote by Richard R. Dupree, former CEO of Procter and Gamble.

"If you leave us our money, our factories and our brands and take away our people, the company will fail. But if you take away our money, our factories and our brand, and leave us our people, we can re-build the whole thing in a decade."

People are a very important asset and we need to respect one another, not considering ourselves as being better in any way. All that we are and all that we have is from God, and we should thank Him for His grace and mercy.

Jesus was a prime example of someone who understood the importance of people and relationships as He delivered the simple message of salvation. In addition, He understood that His source was from God and constantly drew attention to the fact that He said what He heard His Father say, did what He saw His Father do and could not do anything without the Father.

PEOPLE ARE A VERY IMPORTANT ASSET AND WE NEED TO RESPECT ONE ANOTHER

1 Corinthians 4 v 6 – 7 also contributes to the reasons why we should respect one another as people:

Now, brothers, I have applied these things to myself and Apollos for your benefit, so that you may learn from us the meaning of the saying, "Do not go beyond what is written." Then you will not take pride in one man over against another.

For who makes you different from anyone else? What do you have that you did not receive? And if you did receive it, why do you boast as though you did not?

Our prayer should be that the LORD gives us the grace to understand and respect one another.

"HEAR ME OUT"

At a recent conference, the host requested that we should find a partner and highlight areas where we felt we needed improvements. The reaction was two fold – a group of people looked for people that they did not know and the other group looked for people they were comfortable with – for obvious reasons!

I guess in my case, I was lucky because my close friend was nearby and we both had the same issue – "Listening Skills". In my case – sometimes I get so excited about a topic that I can't wait to get the information out of my mouth at the expense of trying to listen and hear the other party but by His grace I am improving.

To be honest – this really shows no respect for the other parties and we are given some insight into it's importance in Proverbs 1 v 5 with a bit of icing on the cake from Proverbs 1 v 33:

"A wise man will hear and increase learning, And a man of understanding will attain wise counsel

But whoever listens to me will dwell safely, And will be secure, without fear of evil."

One of the speakers from the conference made a very important point which sums up the importance of learning to truly listen from the heart:

"Communication is not about communication but about understanding"

INTELLECTUAL CAPITAL

Acquiring degrees to confirm your expertise in a particular subject is good but once it begins to form the basis of all your decisions in terms of intellect – it can pose a problem. After many years, I now know that sometimes you have to put your intellect aside and rely on God regardless of how foolish His advice may seem. Remember that what seems foolish with God is greater than the wisdom of man.

I am not advocating against acquiring "intellectual capital" but total allowance has to be given to God to operate within His own "infinite" parameters. In Luke 10 v 25 - 29, we see Jesus squaring up against the experts in the law – giving them an "advanced" course on what eternal life is about.

On one occasion an expert in the law stood up to test Jesus. "Teacher," he asked, "what must I do to inherit eternal life?" "What is written in the Law?" he replied.

"How do you read it?" He answered: " 'Love the Lord your God with all your heart and with all your soul and with all your strength and with all your mind'; and, 'Love your neighbour as yourself. "You have answered correctly," Jesus replied. "Do this and you will live." But he wanted to justify himself, so he asked Jesus, "And who is my neighbour?"

Jesus did not go to law school but his approach to answering the "so called" experts in the law should be archived in every QC's library. Luke 10 v 36 - 37 gives the summation of his response:

"Which of these three do you think was a neighbor to the man who fell into the hands of robbers?" The expert in the law replied, "The one who had mercy on him." Jesus told him, "Go and do likewise."

We need to realize that a degree is just a tool but the wisdom to apply it comes from the Almighty God.

INTELLIGENCE REPORT

Have you ever acted on advice, and had your actions result in negative consequences?

Have you ever wondered why it did not go your way? I read sometime ago that the mark of a great commander is his ability to make the right decisions, despite the variety of accurate and inaccurate information that falls on his desk.

The information we act on can come from friends, enemies, counsellors, military advisers and so on. Regardless of the source, we have to act on it and bear the consequences. We only have to reflect on the scenario that led to the Iraq war and the fallout to confirm the importance of such information.

In 2 Samuel 10 v 2 - 4, we see the consequences Hanun king of the Ammonites had to bear when he relied on the intelligence reports of his noblemen without weighing up their claims. David meant to show him kindness, but his noblemen - maybe out of insecurity - misinterpreted the kind gesture:

When David's men came to the land of the Ammonites, The Ammonite nobles said to Hanun their lord, "Do you think David is honoring your father by sending men to

you to express sympathy? Hasn't David sent them to you to explore the city and spy it out and overthrow it?" So Hanun seized David's men, shaved off half of each man's beard, cut off their garments in the middle at the buttocks, and sent them away.

I have sometimes made such mistakes and misinterpreted acts of kindness, thinking there was an ulterior motive and acted accordingly. The consequences can be devastating, as we see in one of King David's numerous attacks on the Ammonites in 2 Samuel 11 v 1:

...David sent Joab with the king's men and the whole Israelite army. They destroyed the Ammonites and besieged Rabbah.

Our response to information is crucial if we are going to avoid negative consequences ruining our lives.

The LORD tells us in His Word that we should ask for wisdom. In my opinion, Hanun would have saved himself a lot of hassle if he had tried to decipher the information prior to any action by seeking godly counsel and wisdom.

IT'S WHO YOU KNOW!

Networking is a concept that has been practised for a very long time.

Meeting the right people at the right place at the right time has led to phrases such as 'power dressing', 'power tie', 'power suit' and so on. In addition, the need to join the right health club, golf club, and yacht club has led many to bankruptcy as they attempt to climb the so-called social ladder. Networking as a concept is defined as:

"An extended group of people with similar interests or concerns, who interact and remain in informal contact for mutual assistance or support."

This could explain the need for us to ensure that we meet the right people at the right place and at the right time at all costs. This description got me thinking, 'Who are the right people?', 'Are they in the right place?', and finally, 'Is it the right time to meet them?'

Proverbs 3 v 3 - 4 give us an insight into ensuring that our networking is effective:

Let love and faithfulness never leave you; bind them around your neck, write them on the tablet of your heart.

Then you will win favour and a good name in the sight of God and man.

The favour of God is the effective 'networking' that will ensure we meet the right people at the right place, and at the right time.

I'VE GOT YOUR BACK

At a Couple's dinner event, a question was asked to assess the degree of closeness between husbands and wives.

'Who is your husband's best friend?' On my table, we began to ask ourselves who our best friends are. Based on my understanding I pointed out that I did not have a best friend, but many friends. My answer led those seated at my table into a lengthy discussion on the characteristics of a best friend.

It was quite amusing to see people's reaction when I said a best friend should be ready to die for you. You should be able to say with honesty and loyalty that 'he has got your back', as the Americans would say.

I have seen relationships that were supposed to be based on true friendship dissolve over trivial matters, which leads us to ask, 'Who is a best friend?'

The Bible sheds light on some of the potential characteristics in 2 Samuel 23 v 14 - 17:

At that time David was in the stronghold, and the Philistine garrison was at Bethlehem.

David longed for water and said, "Oh, that someone would get me a drink of water from the well near the gate of Bethlehem!"

So the three mighty men broke through the Philistine lines, drew water from the well near the gate of Bethlehem and carried it back to David. But he refused to drink it; instead, he poured it out before the LORD.

"Far be it from me, O LORD, to do this!" he said. "Is it not the blood of men who went at the risk of their lives?" And David would not drink it. Such were the exploits of the three mighty men.

Now, I ask the question to every one of us – Who is your best friend, and what do you expect from a best friend?

Has your answer remained the same or has it changed?

JUST LISTEN

A crucial area in the utilisation of information is our ability to listen. It is not just enough to hear, we need to go a step further by listening.

Effective communication involves listening, not just hearing.

In hearing, we may perceive the parameters below, and not the essence of the message:

1. Noise
2. Nagging
3. A negative tone
4. An aggressive tone
5. A rude tone.

In listening, we go a step further and try to understand the message behind some of the 'hearing factors' described above.

In listening we ask ourselves the following questions using the following 'starters':

1. Where is this discussion going? - an end picture
2. Who - remember who you are talking to
3. Why - is this issue being discussed?
4. What - is the underlying message?
5. How - is this issue to be solved?

These give a better understanding of the issue at hand and will help you become a better listener.

KNOW THY ENEMY

In the film "The God Father" – Michael Corleone gave a famous quote **"Never hate your enemies, it affects your judgment"**. It is not surprising that our "war counsel" - Jesus Christ advises us to **"love our enemies"**. My understanding of what Michael was trying to point out is that the only way to know the strategy of your enemy and respond accordingly is to be in a rational state of mind. The emotion of hate will not facilitate such a state.

How many times have we allowed negative emotions like anger, hate, and jealousy to affect our judgement on tackling delicate situations? How many times have we lashed out at our friends, families without taking a step back to analyse the situation and make the right judgement.

We are given sound advice in Ephesians 6 v 12 – 13 on who the enemy really is and the effective strategy to apply to make sound judgements:

For our struggle is not against flesh and blood, but against the rulers, against the authorities, against the powers of this dark world and against the spiritual forces of evil in the heavenly realms. Therefore put on the full armor of God, so that when the day of evil comes, you may be able to stand your ground, and after you have done everything, to stand.

Later on in the film, we see Michael telling a family member *"Papa always says "Keep your friends close but your enemies closer"*

As Christians we are in a war and we should not underestimate the wiles of the enemy. We thank God that our weapons are mighty in the power of the Lord.

LEVEL PLAYING FIELD

How many times do we find ourselves passing judgment and looking down on individuals who, in our eyes, are not 'walking the walk'?

We forget that we were once sinners ourselves, and that it is only by grace we stand. There was a time when I used to smoke, womanise and steal – or as we used to say in school to make it sound better – we would say 'I tapped it'. Yes, I used to do those things, and some of my bad habits still remain, but for God!

Inasmuch as there are laws to make us aware of wrong doing, the Bible highlights in Romans 3 v 21 – 24 that we were all once on a level playing field in terms of sin. Thank God for the righteousness that comes from believing in Him:

But now righteousness from God, apart from law, has been made known, to which the Law and the Prophets testify.

This righteousness from God comes through faith in Jesus Christ to all who believe. There is no difference, for all have sinned and fall short of the glory of God, and are justified freely by his grace through the redemption that came by Christ Jesus.

What can wash my sins away? Nothing but the blood of Jesus!

LOVE ISLAND

Insecurity as the word denotes invokes fear of the unknown by an individual. We can see the extent of its hold on people by reviewing some case studies:

- A German leader destroyed 6 million Jews because of his desire for a society that was void of their influence;
- A Ugandan dictator destroyed every one that he thought was in opposition to his government;
- Organizations "pay off" or promote individuals who are opposed to their bad policies on the treatment of junior workers;
- A manager constantly runs down his assistant in public because he fears he will be promoted due to his recent outstanding appraisal.

As you can see from the examples above, insecurity causes people to adopt oppressive measures to alleviate what they see as threats to their well being and existence. Only insecure people see what others do not see so they base their decisions and actions on "false evidence that appears real" – FEAR

In 1 John 4 v 18, we are given the antidote for insecurity:

There is no fear in love. But perfect love drives out fear, because fear has to do with punishment. The one who fears is not made perfect in love.

With the perfection of God's love in us, we need not fear nor feel insecure. His grace is sufficient and we do not fear punishment or judgment. Then we are free to love others.

MINISTERIAL APPOINTMENT

In government or in the church, being appointed as a minister involves taking responsibility for delegated tasks. Delegation means that you have been given the power from your superiors to carry out your responsibility. This power is essential for you to wield your influence in whatever role and portfolio you have been assigned.

Some governments understand the importance of this power and in order to systematically remove an individual from his office – may assign you as a minister without a portfolio. This can be very frustrating as the power and influence to be effective has been taken away.

In addition to being given power and influence, one character a true minister should have to facilitate effectiveness is the commitment to performing your duty with total sacrifice. This may be lacking in some government set up but as Christians 2 Corinthians 6 v 3 – 10 gives us a synopsis of what is required:

We put no stumbling block in anyone's path, so that our ministry will not be discredited. Rather, as servants of God we commend ourselves in every way: in great endurance; in troubles, hardships and distresses; in beatings, imprisonments and riots; in hard work, sleepless nights and hunger; in purity, understanding, patience and kindness; in the Holy Spirit and in sincere love; in truthful speech and in the power of God; with weapons of righteousness in the right hand and in the

left; through glory and dishonor, bad report and good report; genuine, yet regarded as impostors; known, yet regarded as unknown; dying, and yet we live on; beaten, and yet not killed; sorrowful, yet always rejoicing; poor, yet making many rich; having nothing, and yet possessing everything.

What is important is not who you are in terms of "a title" but what you do "sacrificially" to pursue the mandate given to us by God.

OPEN HEART SURGERY

The important role that evangelism plays is highlighted by the various methods that are currently being adopted to attract people to the kingdom of God. Evangelism as a tool is necessary so people can learn how to have a relationship with Jesus.

Just like the marketing of a "product" – church programs are designed to meet the needs of the different people that consist in the church market place. This has led to a plethora of programs – some that are led by the Holy Spirit and some with ulterior motives.

In my opinion, the ultimate objective of every vehicle of evangelism should be to open the people's hearts so they heed to the Word of God. This is possible via prayers hence the need to saturate all programs with heart-led prayers as seen in Acts 16 v 13 - 14:

On the Sabbath we went outside the city gate to the river,
where we expected to find a place of prayer. We sat down
and began to speak to the women who had
gathered there. One of those listening was a woman
named Lydia, a dealer in purple cloth from the city of
Thyatira, who was a worshiper of God. The Lord opened
her heart to respond to Paul's message.

Evangelism should be viewed as a tool which should be
wielded in the power of God which is activated by prayers so
that the hearts of the people are prepared to heed to the
Word of God and apply it to their daily lives.

OPPOSITION LEADER

If your pastor did something wrong, would you have the
courage to confront him or would you just accept the fact
that he is the LORD's anointed and should not be touched?

On the other hand, should we discuss the issue with others
and by so doing, engage in the art of backstabbing?

In my opinion there are two main reasons why an
individual may not confront a pastor or senior official in the
church, namely fear and 'man-pleasing', so as to curry favour
or supposedly remain in the good books of the man of God.

This type of action only hinders the character development
of an individual, as he may be unaware of the error in his
actions. We only need to look at the spate of incidents

involving senior officials in the church, which prompts the question:

Was there no one bold and sincere enough to confront them based on the truth?

In confronting, we need to adopt the approach that Paul used with Peter in Galatians 2 v 11 – 14:

When Peter came to Antioch, I opposed him to his face, because he was clearly in the wrong.

Before certain men came from James, he used to eat with the Gentiles. But when they arrived, he began to draw back and separate himself from the Gentiles because he was afraid of those who belonged to the circumcision group.

The other Jews joined him in his hypocrisy, so that by their hypocrisy even Barnabas was led astray.

When I saw that they were not acting in line with the truth of the gospel, I said to Peter in front of them all, "You are a Jew, yet you live like a Gentile and not like a Jew. How is it, then, that you force Gentiles to follow Jewish customs?"

The Bible tells us in countless ways that only the truth will set us free. Let us adopt the boldness shown by Paul in confronting with love and truth when we see wrong being done.

PARENT TRAP

After attending a talent show put on by the children's church last weekend, I realised there is a massive communication gap between the younger and older generations.

It also explained why there is so much rebellion and frustration in homes, as we find it ever more difficult to understand where our children are coming from.

The reality hit me when I tried to give one of the younger children a 'high five', but instead got a 'fist in the air'. Thankfully, his response did not mean 'Let's get ready to rumble', but apparently, I should have reciprocated by knocking his fist down. I could go on, but I will save myself further embarrassment!

Times have changed, and we should not try to force our children to follow guidelines they do not understand. The same applied in Jesus' day; His mother Mary could not understand it when He asked her why she was worried after he had been 'lost' for three days. After reading that statement, I began to envisage how my own parents would have reacted!

Further probing by Mary and Joseph may have limited their concerns, as we see in Luke 2 v 45 – 49:

When they did not find Him, they went back to Jerusalem to look for Him.

After three days they found Him in the temple courts, sitting among the teachers, listening to them and asking them questions.

Everyone who heard Him was amazed at His understanding and His answers.

When His parents saw Him, they were astonished. His mother said to Him, "Son, why have you treated us like this? Your father and I have been anxiously searching for you."

"Why were you searching for me?" He asked. "Didn't you know I had to be in my Father's house?" But they did not understand what He was saying to them.

I am not advocating the soft touch when relating to or disciplining our children.

But we should take the time to review and understand things from their perspective, so we can react according to the relevant information at hand.

PASSION FRUIT

I heard a message yesterday by one of my spiritual mentors that reminded me of the saying: 'One man's meat (fruit) is another man's poison'.

Have you ever tried to convince people to believe in your vision to the point of frustration? Have you ever wondered why people's reactions to certain events differ to yours?

The bad news is that our attitudes need to change if we react this way. The good news is that the Bible points out the reason why your passion is different from someone else's. It is all about the diverse and different gifts that God has put in us as pointed out in 1 Corinthians 12 v 4 - 6:

There are different kinds of gifts, but the same Spirit.

There are different kinds of service, but the same Lord.

There are different kinds of working, but the same God works all of them in all men.

In my line of work we have clients that may not share our outlook on a solution, so we have been taught to 'manage our client's expectations'.

In other words, manage the client's outlook and guide him rather than trying to forcibly convince him to run with your solution.

If you want someone to share your passion and run with it, you will have to understand and appreciate their gifts. Then you will be able to manage their expectations and understanding of your passion and guide them along the way.

On a final note, you can also take that opportunity to learn about a gift you may not possess, but which could be beneficial to you later on.

QUESTION TIME

As a consultant, I have had the privilege of interacting with colleagues who are experts at communicating during interviews and negotiations with clients.

In order to engage the client in effective conversation, they always use questions to assist the client in exploring the wider scope of issues.

Good communicators go one step further by using questions to answer a question. The advantage of this method, if used effectively, is that it guides the client to understand and provide the answers to their own questions.

We see the art of great communication using questions to answer a question utilised by Jesus in Luke 20 v 22 – 25:

"Is it right for us to pay taxes to Caesar or not?" He saw through their duplicity and said to them, "Show me a denarius. Whose portrait and inscription are on it?" "Caesar's," they replied. He said to them, "Then give to Caesar what is Caesar's, and to God what is God's."

Another example is seen in Luke 7 v 20 – 23:

When the men came to Jesus, they said, "John the Baptist sent us to you to ask, 'Are you the one who was to come, or should we expect someone else?' "

At that very time Jesus cured many who had diseases, sicknesses and evil spirits, and gave sight to many who were blind.

So he replied to the messengers, "Go back and report to John what you have seen and heard: The blind receive sight, the lame walk, those who have leprosy are cured, the deaf hear, the dead are raised, and the good news is preached to the poor. Blessed is the man who does not fall away on account of me."

In other words, Jesus wanted John to answer his own question by observing the wonderful and mighty things He had done, and make his own judgement!

RUNAWAY JURY

To those who read John Grisham novels or watch the films, I would say that Runaway Jury is a classic.

The book and film is about a woman whose husband was shot dead. A million-dollar lawsuit was launched against the gun manufacturer as to the ease with which guns could be obtained.

A jury was selected, and two parties tried to influence their thought patterns. The first party was led by a member of the jury who had lost someone dear through a gun shooting, and the second was led by the defence counsel, who tried to blackmail every member of the jury with information about their past lives. The first party managed to convince the jury to vote against the gun manufacturer, and the prosecution won millions of dollars in compensation for their client.

What made the difference was the approach adopted by both parties in trying to sway the jury. The first party stuck to the facts and empathized with the other jury members when he found out they were being blackmailed. The second party used an aggressive and negative approach which had no lasting impact on the jury.

In trying to convince people to accept the gospel, we need to stick to the facts of the gospel and not try to manipulate people into salvation, as confirmed in Titus 1 v 9 - 11:

He must hold firmly to the trustworthy message as it has been taught, so he can encourage others by sound doctrine and refute those who oppose it.

For there are many rebellious people, mere talkers and deceivers, especially those of the circumcision group.

They must be silenced, because they are ruining whole households by teaching things they ought not to teach – and that for the sake of dishonest gain.

We need to teach the truth so our 'jury' – which is made up of non-Christians - are not put off!

IN TRYING TO CONVINCE PEOPLE TO ACCEPT THE GOSPEL, WE NEED TO STICK TO THE FACTS OF THE GOSPEL AND NOT TRY TO MANIPULATE PEOPLE INTO SALVATION

SPRING CLEANING

I heard once that if you do not wear clothing for up to 3 months – then it does not belong to you. In other words, you should give someone who really needs it.

This statement will gain me a lot of friends on the male front but potential foes on the female side as they will argue strongly that the clothes are in storage for the right occasion.

A lot of lifestyle writers have made money writing books on the art of de-cluttering but I question whether their advice has been heeded as I have had the privilege of a sneak preview of the wardrobes of my blessed wife. In addition, I have been privy to conversations held between my friends and their wonderful wives over this issue of **'Fashion T.V'.** My wonderful daughters have even joined the bandwagon as they spend hours just trying to pick a dress for the so called 'right occasion'.

How do you convince our lovely wives, daughters and sisters on the importance of de-cluttering? Let us consult a section of the ultimate source of insight and wisdom - Luke 3 v 10 – 11:

"What should we do then?" the crowd asked. John answered, "The man with two tunics should share with him who has none, and the one who has food should do the same."

Ladies – are you still my friends after reading this? I hope you are and I wish you all the best as you begin to share your abundance with those who lack – I love you all.

"THAT'S MY BOY"

As I prayed over my son this morning, I began to think about the journey he will take in life.

How will he handle peer pressure, how will he treat women, how will he handle the pressure from society about his stand as a Christian? Will he take the narrow or wide path?

What about his relationship with God? How will he respond to the advice given to him by his parents? Will he desire the Word of God or the word of man?

To conclude, what advice will he give his own son? My daydreaming was halted by my daughters, who needed my advice on what they should have for breakfast!

The Bible highlights a scenario where a dying father is giving his son some fine counsel in 1 Kings 2 v 1 - 4:

When the time drew near for David to die, he gave a charge to Solomon his son.

"I am about to go the way of all the earth," he said. "So be strong, show yourself a man, and observe what the LORD your God requires: Walk in his ways, and keep his decrees and commands, his laws and requirements, as written in the Law of Moses, so that you may prosper in all you do and wherever you go,

and that the LORD may keep his promise to me: 'If your descendants watch how they live, and if they walk faithfully before me with all their heart and soul, you will never fail to have a man on the throne of Israel.'

As parents, the best we can do for our children is to give them godly advice, because we cannot be with them 24/7. The advice we give will form the foundation upon which they journey through life.

THE ACCUSER

One of the greatest cop-out phrases used by individuals is 'It was the devil'. This blame culture started in the Garden of Eden.

If my theology serves me right, only God is omnipresent, and so the devil lacks the ability to be everywhere at once. It is so convenient to blame what we cannot see or seemingly confront.

I heard a conversation yesterday where all manner of accusations was levelled against the enemy. I was amazed that the individual could not see it was not the devil's fault, but that errors were due to lack of commitment and a failure to take ownership for the decisions made.

On the flip side, the Bible labels the devil - and not us - as 'The accuser of all brethren'. As a result we should be careful how involved we get in the accusing business, as we blame everything on the devil and risk reflecting his characteristics.

This is nowhere highlighted more than in Jude v 8 – 10:

In the very same way, these dreamers pollute their own bodies, reject authority and slander celestial beings.

But even the archangel Michael, when he was disputing with the devil about the body of Moses, did not dare to bring a slanderous accusation against him, but said, "The Lord rebuke you!"

Yet these men speak abusively against whatever they do not understand; and what things they do understand by

instinct, like unreasoning animals - these are the very things that destroy them.

Even the angels' equivalent of a five-star general did not utter an accusing word at the enemy!

We need to understand situations before passing comments. It is not always the devil; we need to weigh our actions in respect to the Word of God.

Finally, seek the insight and revelation you need from God about all situations that occur in your life, and avoid the shot-gun approach.

THE ANIMAL KINGDOM

How many of you watch programs about the behaviour of animals. Such amazing insight and confirmation of why God uses animals to explain principles and concepts.

I attended a service where "the animal kingdom" was used to give us detailed insight into the art of spiritual warfare. The case study was taken from Matthew 10 v 16:

Behold, I send you out as sheep in the midst of wolves. Therefore be wise as serpents and harmless as doves.

Highlighted below are the characteristics of each animal which facilitates a greater understanding of the art of spiritual warfare:

Wolves:
1 Skillful and Cunning
2. Move Silently
3. Look for sheep when they are eating grass (or most
   vulnerable or likened to a Christian that is too focused
   on the blessing of God and not being aware of the
   surrounding environment)

Dove:
1. Pure in Heart
2. No Hidden Agenda
3. Gentle
4. Innocent and Sincere
5. Tender and Simple

Serpent:
1 Does not expose himself unnecessarily
2 Only exposes himself when required –
   (*do not share your testimony/information with everyone*)
3. Very Patient
4. Tough Minded
5. Focused
6. Identifies and isolates a goal
7. Extremely aware of his situation and circumstances

May God give us the heart of a dove but the mindset of a
serpent.

THE FIRST IMPRESSION

Organizations lay a lot of emphasis on the operations of their customer service departments.

They have realised that this point of contact is crucial for customer retention, and determines whether a person remains a 'loyal' customer or just a 'one-off' customer. Most referrals to utilise an organisation's products or services are based on our recommendations to friends, families and those in our spheres of influence, hence the importance of us having a memorable experience with an organisation.

I once went to visit a client to conduct a review of their business processes. After the initial meeting, I pointed out that my first experience of getting in contact with them had not been a memorable one.

The meeting was scheduled for 3.00pm and on arrival at their offices there was no sign a meeting was going to hold as numerous calls were not answered. On getting to the location, an unscheduled meeting was being held and I was asked to sit down at a nearby desk. It was only after the meeting that an apology was proffered.

The importance of how we speak and behave towards others is highlighted in Colossians 4 v 5 - 6:

Be wise in the way you act toward outsiders; make the most of every opportunity.

Let your conversation be always full of grace, seasoned with salt, so that you may know how to answer everyone.

THREE WISE MEN

I was reminiscing about my life yesterday and how God has taken me into my current profession and I was amazed at the way he has done this. Most of them have been by "divine" association and placement.

I studied for an MBA because a friend was studying for his degree and I thought to myself that it won't be a bad idea without even reading or understanding what was involved in pursuing this type of course.

I got into my line of specialisation after a company wide reshuffle and a Manager approached me if I would like to go to the United States to study a subject I had not even heard about.

God is truly amazing and his advice in Proverbs 13 v 20 gives us a further insight into the power of association:

He who walks with the wise grows wise, but a companion of fools suffers harm

Please note that I am not advocating that you do not study to show yourself approved and understand the decisions you have to make – the point of this story is to highlight God's mercy and favour upon our lives. God is truly the Master strategist, placing people at the right place – at the right time and with the right people.

VALUE CHAIN

Work-life balance has become one of the main focuses of the business world.

Organisations are beginning to realise that the health and welfare of their staff is crucial to maintain productivity and reduce absenteeism due to sickness and fatigue.

On the way back from an event I began to ponder on this, and why we have to work long hours to achieve results. What is even more interesting is that as we climb the corporate ladder, the less work we seem to do in terms of being "hands on", and the more work we seem to do in the area of "networking" with clients.

All in all, we spend too much time at work, sometimes to the detriment of our relationship with our families and loved ones.

VALUE CREATION IS WHAT GUARANTEES AN INCREASE IN OUR PRODUCTIVITY AND INCOME.

A speaker at a conference highlighted one of the reasons why total reliance on overtime is not such a good concept. He pointed out that he used to work for one hour and earn $5. Now he works for an hour and could earn up to $5,000. The difference is not in the amount of time spent on the tasks, since both jobs were for an hour. The difference is in the value of the work being performed. If you produce value in the time you have, there will be no need to rely on overtime to complete the allotted tasks.

Please do not get me wrong, overtime is necessary at certain phases of our lives, but in the long run value creation is what guarantees an increase in our productivity and income.

Jesus spent thirty-three years on earth, which is about half our predicted lifespan. He achieved more in His short life than anyone would in a lifetime and at the end of it all, He could confirm the completion of His tasks in John 19 v 30:

When He had received the drink, Jesus said, "It is finished."

UNITED WE STAND, DIVIDED WE FALL

Arsenal, Manchester United, Chelsea, the Australian Cricket team, the McLaren racing team, and the Chicago Bulls basketball team all have one common trait that has guaranteed them success over the years - TEAMWORK.

Every leader knows that if you can get people working as one unit, pursuing the same purpose and vision, success is generally guaranteed. I have observed countless times where coaches have used half-time intervals to encourage and motivate their players to work as a unit, so as to reduce and offset any deficit created during the initial period of play.

The importance of having a mindset of unity within a team and facilitating effective teamwork is highlighted in 1 Corinthians 1 v 10:

I appeal to you, brothers, in the name of our Lord Jesus Christ, that all of you agree with one another so that there may be no divisions among you and that you may be perfectly united in mind and thought.

As the Scripture points out, creating an atmosphere of unity is first initiated in our minds and thoughts before being manifested by our actions. Jesus understood the importance of fostering unity. Prior to His departure He prayed to God that we remain as one, as seen in John 17 v 11:

I will remain in the world no longer, but they are still in the world, and I am coming to you. Holy Father, protect them by the power of your name - the name you gave me - so that they may be one as we are one.

UNTIL THAT DAY

I often wonder why we sometimes behave and react differently to other individuals who do not think, talk and act like us.

Surely, there is a common denominator that makes us all the same, regardless of colour, tribe or creed? In my opinion, this is undoubtedly one of the main reasons why there is so much war in the world the fact that we do not see eye to eye, and often require an intermediary to settle disputes. Thank God for the Great Intermediary – Jesus.

I remember some inspiring lyrics from Bob Marley that reflects this notion:

Until the philosophy that holds one race superior than another;
Until the colour of a man's skin is of no more significance than the colour of his eyes;
Until the basic human rights is equally guaranteed to all without regards to race.
Until that day – the dream of lasting peace, world citizenship and the rule of international morality – shall remain but a fleeting illusion to be pursued.
Until that day – there will be war and rumours of war.

That day, in my opinion, will be when Jesus returns. Prior to that, we have to remember that we are all the same, and we need to learn to live with one another regardless of our differences.

The common denominator that makes us the same is God's breath of life, which was put in Adam prior to his mission to be fruitful and multiply as indicated in Genesis 1 v 27:

So God created man in His own image,
in the image of God He created him;
male and female He created them.

The gift of freewill given to us by God is the vehicle that man uses to go in a different direction.

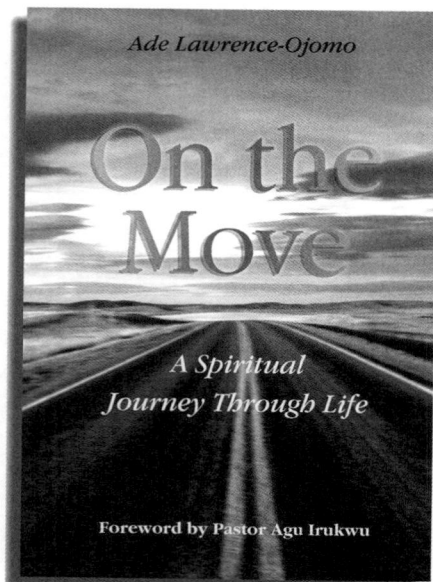